Out of the Ashes

OUT OF THE ASHES
REBUILDING AMERICAN CULTURE

ANTHONY ESOLEN

REGNERY
PUBLISHING
A Division of Salem Media Group

Regnery® is a registered trademark of Salem Communications Holding Corporation

Cataloging-in-Publication data on file with the Library of Congress

ISBN 978-1-62157-514-6

Published in the United States by
Regnery Publishing
A Division of Salem Media Group
300 New Jersey Ave NW
Washington, DC 20001
www.Regnery.com

Manufactured in the United States of America

10 9 8 7 6 5 4 3 2 1

Books are available in quantity for promotional or premium use. For information on discounts and terms, please visit our website: www.Regnery.com.

Distributed to the trade by
Perseus Distribution
www.perseusdistribution.com

Also by Anthony Esolen

Ten Ways to Destroy the Imagination of Your Child

Ironies of Faith: The Laughter at the Heart of Christian Literature

The Politically Incorrect Guide® to Western Civilization

Reflections on the Christian Life: How Our Story is God's Story

Living the Days of Advent and the Christmas Season

Reclaiming Catholic Social Teaching

Defending Marriage: Twelve Arguments for Sanity

*Life Under Compulsion: Ten Ways to Destroy the
Humanity of Your Child*

Jerusalem Delivered

The Divine Comedy (translator)

On the Nature of Things (translator)

CONTENTS

The Rubble

In this book I shall indulge myself in one of civilized man's most cherished privileges. I shall decry the decay of civilization.

I stand with Livy, who at the final hardening of Rome's republican arteries, wrote that the study of his land's history was the study of the rise and fall of moral strength, with duty and severity giving way to ambition, avarice, and license, till his fellow Romans "sank lower and lower, and finally began the downward plunge which has brought us to the present time, when we can endure neither our vices nor their cure."

My heart goes out to the exile Dante, who loved his native city of Florence, with its old aristocratic modesty and gentility, and hated what it had become, a bustling center of money-making and bloodthirsty politics. Thus he has his great-great-grandfather, Cacciaguida, in Paradise, like any old Italian man rocking on his front stoop to this day, say of his now long-forgotten fellows:

With these
and others I saw Florence in repose,
never a cause to shed a tear. With these
I saw them lead a just and glorious life,
townsmen who never saw some victor drag
their lily backward in the field, nor strife
Of party turn it red upon the flag.

Or I walk with the ancient Saxon poet of "The Wanderer," whose principal experience in this world is the loss of what was once full of vigor and glory and gladness:

He who thus wisely considers this wall, the world,
and into our dark life casts his mind deep,
his heart old and keen, calls back from long ago
that wealth of slaughters, and utters these words:
"Where has the horse gone? Where has the hero? Where are
the hall-joys?
Where the giver of gems? Where the gathering for feasts?
Alas, the bright goblet! Alas, the burnished mail!
Alas, the prince's power! How that time has passed,
now dim under the night-helm, as if it never were!"

After Rome was sacked in 410 by a frustrated glory-seeker, the German warlord Alaric, Saint Jerome wrote, "Who would believe that Rome, built up by the conquest of the whole world, had collapsed, that the mother of nations had become also their tomb?" I might say now, "Who would believe that the whole Western world, in whose image, for better or for worse, all nations seemed to hurry to refashion themselves, would collapse, not battered from without, but sagging into lethargy and indifference and stupor from within?"

Are the words too harsh?

Let me anticipate an objection that my own citations above must provoke. "People are always complaining about decline and fall," someone will say, "but that does not mean that things are actually as bad as they believe. It is simply one generation's way of complaining about the next. You are an inveterate *laudator temporis acti,* one who praises the time gone by, forgetting its evils and overlooking the virtues of the present age."

There are two answers to the charge. One is that in any civilization, at any time, there will be some good things in decline, and so we will always need people who pull us up short, and say, "Perhaps the amalgamation of family farms into vast tracts of agribusiness is not an *entirely* good thing," or, "Perhaps the nearly universal exodus of women from homes and neighborhoods into offices does not bode well for the homes and neighborhoods, and that is something we should consider." In itself the radio is a wonderful thing, bringing great music and pleasant entertainment into millions of homes. It also precipitated the decay of music *made by people themselves,* from printed scores, from folk memories passed down over the centuries, and from sheer quirky inventiveness. In itself the television is a wonderful thing—why, you might watch a special on emperor penguins of the Antarctic and see the big fellows waddling about the ice, diving into the cold seas to fish, or settling their large eggs between their feet to keep them warm. But you may more likely waste countless hours in half-attention and not even know the name of that cheerful little gray bird with the crest pecking at the bark of some tree or other ten feet from your window.

More people *watch* baseball than ever before, in high-tech stadia, prickly with electronic pictures and lights and noise that are meant to be like injections of adrenaline, over and over. Fewer people play it. Every small town in the country once boasted its own baseball team; plenty of factories did, too. All that is gone, and nothing in a town's common life has come to replace it. Rather, most of the things that were like it—town bands, playhouses, choirs, block parties, founders' days, and so forth— are gone, too.

So there will always be some justification for those who warn about things passing away. But the second answer to the charge of exaggeration or intransigent nostalgia is more powerful. *Sometimes entire civilizations do decay and die, and the people who point that out are correct.*

Think of the incomparably lively centuries when the city-states of Greece were at their height, when the lyric poet Pindar, profoundly religious, wrote odes in honor of triumphant boys and men at the games of Olympus or Delphi, celebrating not a mere individual achievement, but the very history of the lad's city and family, in the context of the ever-suggestive stories of the gods; when Athens *invented drama itself,* and Aeschylus, in the context of the new Athenian democracy, composed the *Oresteia,* the unsurpassed trilogy of blood-guilt and revenge, of dark passions that we must never ignore, of reasoned argument and the chance, never a certainty, that men can see through the murk of rage and selfishness and come to the straight and just decision. It was when the great statesman Pericles commissioned the building of the Parthenon, that clean and gleaming colonnade of Greek devotion and celebration— now in ruins, thanks to the Turks, who used it for an ammunition cache, exactly as if someone were to use the Bayeux Tapestry for a throw rug.

But having reached her peak, Athens was then absorbed into the empires of Philip of Macedon and his son Alexander and, two centuries later, Rome. She was still the schoolmistress of the Mediterranean world, even after her arts went into decline. The people of the ancient world came before the modern watershed: that which encourages us to believe that what is current must be superior to what is past. We apply what we see in the progress of technology to all other human endeavors, and fail to ask whether technological innovations themselves are always unmixed blessings, let alone whether, for example, modern art with its inhuman abstraction or its deliberate ugliness is really an advancement over what the great tradition had bequeathed to us. Modernity is all too often a cult of erasure and oblivion. The ancients still had memory.

They needed it, too. When the monks of the Rule of Saint Benedict built their monasteries across Europe, planting them even in the dark pagan forests of northern Germany and Ireland and England, they were outposts of memory. You might think that Christian monks would scorn the pagan past, trusting in an endless supercession. "What has Athens to do with Jerusalem?" asked Tertullian, and "What has Ingeld to do with Christ?" asked Alcuin of his monks in the time of Charlemagne when he found them still delighting in the heroic German sagas of old. But those memories lay like seeds in a fertile land in winter and would spring forth in a wholly new genre of song and story, the romances of Christian chivalry, of Arthur and Lancelot, of Roland and Oliver, of Tristan and Percival and Galahad.

Winter comes and goes in the affairs of men and nations and cultures, and if they are to survive at all they must plant seeds: they must remember. What happens if they neglect the planting?

Imagine a great manor house. The Weston family lives here.

First let us see the rooms.

We enter a spacious drawing room, with a great fireplace in the center and portraits of the family patriarchs and matriarchs on the wall. They have grown dark and dull with age. Soot from the fireplace and smoke from cigarettes have turned a scarlet sash to rusty brown and a bright green bonnet to something the color of lichen on the north side of a rock. Sir Peter Weston bears a whitish streak extending from his left eye to what looks like a medal on his chest. It could be the remains of oyster stew that one of the Weston boys flung at him in disgust. It could be bird droppings—for there are strange water stains in one corner of the ceiling, and it appears that the plaster there has long been pecked away. On each frame a silver plaque, tarnished black from sulfur in the air and from neglect, bears the now unreadable name of the portrait's subject. Not one member of the current Weston household can tell you anything about the people up above, except that Lady Amelia was a feminist before her time, because she used to sneak out of the manor to carry on with a plowman in the village, and that Sir Pedicure led a Boy Scout troop with rather more interest than he should have, and that Miss Emmeline made a killing in the Caribbean slave trade, and so on; a few things tawdry, despicable, petty, gross, vile, stupid, and nasty; most of it exaggerated, and some of it downright falsehood.

Then we enter the library, with its high ceiling and large windows to the east and south and west that flood the room with light all hours of the day. A movable ladder on wheels runs along a track set eight feet from the floor, to allow access to a gallery that divides the lower half of the room from the upper half. Lord John Henry Weston, two hundred years ago, had the room built in this way. The lower half is stocked with books in several of the modern languages of Europe. They include novels, collections of poetry, histories, biographies, travelogues, and so forth. If you're a nine-year-old boy and you want to read *Humphry Clinker* or *Robinson Crusoe,* or if you're a little older and you want to read Pope's translation of the *Iliad,* you can find them ready to hand. Or you can get lost there on purpose, as you might go forth into the woods on a sunny day, not knowing where the path will take you.

Lord John Henry devoted the upper half of the room to the upper half of knowledge and culture. There we find works in the ancient languages, Latin and Greek, and books dealing with philosophy, divinity, political constitutions, law, and natural science. The sermons of Lancelot Andrewes are there, near Erasmus's edition of the New Testament in Greek and Hooker's *Ecclesiastical Polity.* The legal writings of Coke and Blackstone are there, near Justinian's *Corpus Juris Civilis* and the works of the Roman jurist Ulpian. Montesquieu, Bossuet, Pufendorf, and Grotius are there, and not just for decoration. Plutarch is there in the original Greek and in North's sixteenth-century English translation. Homer, Virgil, Ovid, Horace, Hesiod—all the poets are there; the Hebrew Bible; various works by Augustine, Chrysostom, Gregory of Nyssa, Lactantius, Jerome. It was the library of a learned man interested in everything human and divine.

If you moved that ladder now, you would notice, in the channels of its wheels, a thick coating of grime and mold. There was a bad storm fifty years ago, and rain began to seep through some broken shingles on the roof, dripping down to the plaster ceiling. One corner of the room is quite gray-green with mildew. No one has done anything about it. If you open that edition of Horace from the Aldine Press, you will be greeted with a dank smell. Spots have begun to appear on the books wherever paper was exposed to the air. You let your hand rest on one of the shelves but then whisk it away at once, when you feel a strange grit lying all about—mouse dirt. In fact, some of the spines of the books have been gnawed through.

The library is not abandoned entirely, though. In one corner there's a table heaped with glossy hardcover biographies of celebrities, like Elvis Presley and Jim Morrison. That's also where the most recent children in the Weston family have stashed their old schoolbooks. Lately the family has taken to using the room for storage, so we also find, crushed against one another, old hat racks, trunks full of outworn clothing, souvenirs from a trip to Disneyland, a sideboard that was supposed to have been repaired but never was, and photo albums filled with pictures of people no one can any longer identify.

Then we go to the conservatory. It's a pleasant sunny room, where the women of the Weston family spent many a happy hour. Believe it or not, there are still forty or fifty jars of conserves in a cabinet there, but nobody has touched them in many years. Nobody really knows any longer what is in them, and if you told them, they still wouldn't know. What is "shagberry," anyway? There is also a baby grand piano and shelves full of sheet music. The strings of the piano have been left untuned for so long their tension has slowly warped the frame meant to hold them, so that now the instrument is irreparable. Many years ago a Master Roland Weston decided to pound the keys with his fist to see what would happen. What happened was that he broke some of the carpentry, so that several of the keys simply lie flat, disconnected from their hammers. Master Roland got a pasting for that, but the piano was left as it was. Thousands of pages of music, most of it purchased from music stores and music publishers one song at a time, lie about collecting dust and dead flies. The Weston women used to play it all the time. No one can read it now.

Should we go to the ballroom? Lady Georgina Weston had it renovated with an art deco coffered ceiling, fashioned by a local Italian carpenter with a knack for floral designs. There is a stage at one end for the musicians. That is also where the Westons would occasionally put on a puppet show for the children. Nobody had any idea that the dances they all had learned from the time they were just little boys and girls would one day have faded from memory. It is true that a current Miss Jasmyn Weston takes lessons in modern jazz dance at a local studio; her movements are like those Salome might have performed before her lecherous stepfather, Herod, if Salome were a little less chaste and decorous. You can, of course, learn how to dance the old dances if you take a special course offered by a local dancing master with a taste running to the antique. It's as if a boy could still learn how to play baseball if he went to a special baseball camp, or as if we all could still learn how to converse with our neighbors if we went on a special conversation retreat.

Then there's the chapel. I need say no more.

That's a private home. Do we want to go out in public?

I will now describe things I have seen with my own eyes.

Here is a state park that used to be thronged with people on a sunny weekend. I have seen photographs of the parking lot from sixty years ago. It features a strange geological phenomenon, the largest such in the world. You don't want to go there now. The nervous man in the lone car in the lot is waiting for an assignation that has to do with either of two things. One of those is drugs, and the other one isn't.

Here is a little grassy "park" with a nice bench and a flowerbed, set aside as a memorial to the high school that used to stand there. It isn't that they built a new school somewhere else. Several towns consolidated their school districts into one and built a massive holding tank far from where anybody lives. Here is a building that used to be a Catholic parochial school. But the order of nuns who used to teach there were infected by a vicious strain of feminism, and the people of the parish could not afford to pay, or did not want to pay, the salaries of the lay teachers who had to replace them. The school, built by the very hands of the grandfathers of those parishioners, now serves for borough offices, complete with a jail. Here is a room in a Catholic high school. Its closet is filled with books in French and German. They have not been opened in forty years, and German is no longer taught there. Here is a church sold off to people who have turned it into a mattress warehouse. Here is a sandlot where boys used to play ball without adult supervision. You would never know that now.

Here is a playground built twenty years too late, so that by the time the land was cleared, the children who would have played there were grown up, and there weren't any children to replace them, because people no longer have any, and the few they do have spend their hours in the company of their principal playmate and instructor, the television—or the computer, or the video game.

Here is what used to be the city's vocational high school, for boys who wanted to learn a trade. It's gone. This is the American Legion building, which used to be the terminus for the town's grand Memorial Day parade. There has not been a parade in fifty years. This is a bandstand, for what used to be the town band. There is no town band. This is what used to be a parish hall, built by a priest with his own family money; it had a library, a billiard room, a gym, and a place for refreshments. It is gone, and nothing like it is in its place. This is a ball field, where the town's baseball team—men, not boys—used to play against teams from other towns. There is no team. There aren't really any towns, either, not if a town implies a community life. Here is a dam where older kids used to swim on summer days. No one swims there now. Here is a privately owned lake that used to sport pavilions for big family outings—for aunts and uncles and cousins. There are no more big family outings.

Enough. If tradition is the handing on of cultural and artisanal knowledge, and if we have taught ourselves in our smugness that we can dispense with it, then we will become cultural and artisanal incompetents. Your grandfather might be a repository of many generations of know-how—and I am not speaking principally of technological know-how. If you will not learn from him, from whom will you learn what he knows—from the pimply teenager next door? Inane actors on television? Teachers whose credentials are mainly in the new and improved Methods for Teaching but who do not know the subject they are supposed to teach? Newspapers? Advertisements on the walls of a bus? Politicians? Bubble gum cards?

Sometimes the name of a thing remains long after the essence has been lost. In that case, people will still say that they do this or that, without knowing that in large part it is no longer true. People still get married, for example. Not many, as it turns out. Unmarried men who shack up with women tend to be irresponsible, unproductive, and aggressive;

unmarried women who shack up with men tend to be selfish and prodigal and to want Big Daddy the government to take the same care of them that fathers and husbands used to take. But those who do marry no longer seem to know what it is that they are doing. Is it for keeps, or not? What happens when children start arriving? What's a husband supposed to do? What's a wife supposed to do?

We are incompetent in the ordinary things of life. We divorce more readily than we sell houses, yet for some reason we believe that we possess great wisdom as regards men and women that our benighted ancestors did not possess. We raise sons who are not weaned at age twenty-five, yet for some reason we have contempt for the old institutions that used to turn boys into men. We raise daughters who emulate well-paid whores, but who do not actually make the money that the whores make, and yet we persist in believing that only in our time has a girl had half a chance to live a decent life. We are in debt over the eyeballs, we cannot make ends meet even on two incomes, and yet we hug ourselves for being "liberated," looking with pity on a grandmother who in a single day did fifty skillful things for people she loved, rather than spending eight hours fielding phone calls in an office or scraping plaque off the teeth of strangers, while wearing goggles and a face mask to guard against dreadful infections from their blood and spittle.

Every single pagan philosopher of the ancient world said that if you wanted to be free, you had to learn the hard ways of virtue and that the worst form of slavery was slavery to your own appetites. That is what the founders of the United States also believed. That is what Christian preachers used to preach. That is what we have repudiated or forgotten, so that now we look to a massive central government for everything. It tells you what proportion of male and female athletes you have to have in your school. It tells you that you have to buy a certain form of medical insurance. It tells you that you have to bake a cake to help sodomites celebrate their mock marriage. It now bids fair to tell you what toilet you have to let a transvestite use—or a transvestite "inside," a man wearing men's clothing on the outside but a frilly skirt on the inside, in his "identity," a wraith conjured up by his own imagination. It tells you what you may say and what you may not say, on pain of being prosecuted for hate—not for an act, but for an attitude.

If your uncle gives you a magnificent Rolls-Royce, and a year later he wants to see how you have done with it, and you show him a tangled mess of metal and rubber, caused not by a freak accident but by your habitual misuse, he will naturally conclude that you are incompetent to own a Rolls-Royce. We were given a republic that guaranteed a wide berth for liberty and for local oversight of local matters, with the central government reserved only for matters that were truly national. We now have what every single one of the founders, federalists and anti-federalists both, would have considered tyrannical. It is a tangled mess.

So we need to clear out the garbage, admit our errors, and rebuild. That requires humility, patience, and determination. But nothing else will do. When your only choices are repentance or oblivion, you repent. It is time to get to work, and that is what this book is about.

ONE

GIVING THINGS THEIR PROPER NAMES:
The Restoration of Truth-Telling

When the Lord God had made *ha adam*, the Man, out of the dust of the earth, He brought to him all the living creatures one by one, and whatever the Man would name them, that would be its name. It is a delightful and extraordinary moment. God has spoken the universe into being, and has declared it all good, very good, and has consummated His creation by establishing the joyous Sabbath. It suggests that the pulsing heart of the universe is a liturgy, a worship-work.

And then the Lord, who has made Man in His own image and likeness and given him dominion over all of the creatures He has made, now gives him his first opportunity to exercise that dominion. Granted, it is not the same thing to name the creatures as to create them, but in giving them their names, man enters into an intellectual and aesthetic and personal relationship with them. It is the first instance of language and art. Adam names them according to what he sees in them: *he calls them*. The Creator allows His creature to be a poet, a "maker," and Adam's act of naming is not arbitrary or tyrannical or demonic or deceitful, but true.

We know what happens soon after. The first temptation is a bald lie, a corruption of words. It is the first example of indirection: "And hath God said?" the serpent says to Eve, with mock incredulity and a feint towards sympathy with man, attributing deceit to God Himself. Our original sin, as the sacred author presents it, is not that we were taught how to make fire, which was why Zeus punished Prometheus, or that we were making too much noise for the petty gods to bear, which was why the Mesopotamian deities decided to drown us all in a great flood. Our original sin was a failure to see things as they were. It was to believe a lie. If the shrewd Confucius is right, that the beginning of wisdom is to give things their proper names, then the beginning of folly is to put any stock in the wrong names.

We have no choice now but to live in a world whose governments and most successful businesses are mills for the mass production of deceit. Aleksandr Solzhenitsyn lived in a particularly horrible deceit-mill, the Soviet Union. Their lies sent him to the Gulag labor camps in Siberia. To suffer persecution at the hands of the liars is one thing. But to live the lie is another. We must not only refuse to give credit to the lie. We—and our children—must refuse to utter the lie, *or to use its language.*

Why Do We Lie?

No one ever takes a picture of his son's first lie.

Why does the child lie? We all know. He lies because he broke the cookie jar when his mother told him to leave it alone. She lies because she teased her baby sister and made her cry, when her mother told her to be nice. Children lie to hide the bad things they have done. So does everyone else.

When Adam and Eve have eaten the fruit of the forbidden tree, they feel for the first time that they must *obstruct* knowledge, that they must obfuscate. They begin by concealing themselves from one another, and then they try to hide from God. Their language is indirect. Adam first passes the blame to Eve, perhaps hoping that all the punishment will light upon her and insinuating that God was to blame for making her in the first place. Then Eve passes the blame to the serpent. Milton sums up their state in words whose concentrated insight is unsurpassed:

> Up they rose
> As from unrest; and each the other viewing,
> Soon found their eyes how opened, and their minds
> How darkened; innocence, that as a veil
> Had shadowed them from knowing ill, was gone;
> Just confidence, and native righteousness,
> And honor from about them, naked left
> To guilty shame: he covered, but his robe
> Uncovered more.

The most revealing thing about us is that we conceal: we tell lies.

We tell them to hide from others and ourselves our wrongs and our failures. We tell them to manipulate and fool others into doing what we want. We tell them to destroy our enemies. And then the lie enters the common language like a small cancer, growing quietly and assimilating what should have been healthy tissue to itself. We must not tell lies. We must not even speak the lie's language.

This is no simple matter. Sincerity has nothing to do with it. Adolf Hitler was sincere: he believed what he said, and he was still one of the most thorough liars in the twentieth century, which is saying a great deal. That is because the lie had coiled itself around the convolutions of his mind, so that he could no longer distinguish truth from falsehood. Most slogans are lies, as George Orwell tried to teach us. Orwell understood that the foundation of tyranny is the corruption of language. He knew whereof he spoke. During the war he worked at the British Broadcasting Corporation, an experience he then used as the basis for the Ministry of Truth in his novel *Nineteen Eighty-Four*. The Ministry of Truth is in the business of destroying evidence of things that have actually happened, sending it down the "memory hole," and crafting cunning lies in debased and simplistic language for widespread consumption by viewers of the state-controlled television. Journalism, that is.

Malcolm Muggeridge, a friend of Orwell and a truth-teller also, wondered in a bemused way what the English Left would do after the Ribbentrop-Molotov accord, when it became known that the Russians were aiding and abetting Hitler and the Nazis. Would they then disown the Soviets? Would they experience a crisis of conscience? How long would that crisis last? A day or two, it seems. They flipped on a dime: Hitler and the Nazis were now not so bad after all. When the Russians and Hitler fell out, and the Russians joined the Allies, then they flipped again. Orwell put it nicely in *Nineteen Eighty-Four*. A government speaker is literally in mid-oration, about to condemn the enemy, Eurasia, when somebody runs up to him and delivers him a written message. He reads it and revises his speech accordingly: Eastasia is the enemy, and Eurasia is the ally. Oceania is at war with Eastasia: Oceania *has always* been at war with Eastasia. And he actually believes what he is saying. That is the lie at its most potent. It is the snake in the brain.

Of course, so long as we remain human, we must still have in us some sense of the truth, however choked or smothered it may be. Then the lie involves a suppression or perversion of our very humanity. A still small voice within whispers to us, "It is not true. You know it is not true. Oceania has *not* always been at war with Eastasia. Two and two *do not* make five. A child is *not* better off at a day care center where no one loves him than at home with his mother. Watching porn is *not* mere recreation. Your vote *does not* have any more impact than that of a grain of sand against a cliff. A life in which you do not know your neighbors *is not* more human than what your grandparents enjoyed." And so forth. The still small voice must be drowned out under noise. The louder and more persistent the lie, the more egregious is its falsehood. People do not host parades to celebrate parking in a no-parking zone.

We must not accept the terms of the lies. A few of us may have to speak in the lie's argot just to engage the liars and the gulled in conversation. The rest of us should not speak or think in it at all. We want neither to manipulate nor to be manipulated. We want to acknowledge our wrongs, an acknowledgment that presumes that there are wrongs, and that there is a moral truth independent of our judgment, to which we must conform ourselves.

Are We a World of Liars?

In a word, yes.

It is almost impossible in the modern world *not to accept lies* as a matter of course. We are told that a woman can make as good a soldier as a man. Except for the rare amazon, that is a lie. Americans are told, by justices whose business it is to know the truth, that the Constitution forbids capital punishment (it presumes that capital punishment will be exacted for certain kinds of crime), that the Constitution forbids prayer to open a public meeting (the drafters of the Constitution began their meetings with prayer), that the Constitution upholds a right of privacy in matters sexual (the Constitution does not mention "privacy" at all), that the Constitution allows Congress to pass laws requiring individuals to make certain purchases for their own good (the drafters of the Constitution had a word for that sort of thing; it was "tyranny"), and so on. The justices know quite well that it is all an elaborate pretense. They know they are building falsehoods upon falsehoods. Justice Sandra Day O'Connor once admitted that the notorious *Roe v. Wade* decision legalizing abortion across the land was decided incorrectly, but she was loath to take back the lie. We had to continue to pretend that it really *was* a constitutionally licit decision, even though it was not, because a generation of women had predicated their economic lives upon it. In other words, lies apparently shade into truth with age. Or lies become truth when they come with the goods.

Actually, they do no such thing. With age, the lies show themselves to be more hoary and monstrous than ever, and that is why you have to lie more flagrantly, to cover yourself for the lies you have already told and do not want to retract. "Sin will pluck on sin," says Macbeth, deeper in evil than he had ever intended to be. The goods they seem to deliver come with hooks and barbs.

I am a Roman Catholic. The essence of what I am to believe is contained in the Nicene Creed, which I can recite at a reflective pace in one minute. Our world today is far more demanding than the bishops at Nicaea were. I am to believe a vast array of outlandish lies, and woe unto me if I do not bend the knee and kiss the liar's sandal! "Family structure doesn't matter." "Sex is biological, but gender is social." "The feminist movement is about equal opportunities for women." "The Indians were peace-loving people, close to nature, and benevolent to everyone." "The world is now warmer than it has ever been, and we are all going to fry like eggs on a skillet unless we cede control over all actions that use up energy"—which is to say, all human actions whatsoever—"to a centralized world bureaucracy." "Religion is the cause of almost all wars." "A million people were burnt at the stake in the Middle Ages."

It isn't just the sheer multitude of the lies, or their weight, like a mudslide rumbling down the side of a two-mile-high volcano. It is that we really do not expect people to do anything but lie. As I write these words, Hillary Clinton, probably the most vulgar, insecure, vindictive, and malevolent human being ever to be nominated by a major party for the presidency, seems to have a better than even chance of winning the office. That is despite a long career of lying in the most outrageous and the pettiest ways. Perhaps her most stunningly inhuman lie came—for she has been lying for so long, it is hard to attribute conscious agency to her—*came,* I say, on the morning after the murders of American diplomats in Benghazi, when she gave the mother of one of the murdered soldiers a straight look and assured her that a certain insignificant filmmaker in California, who she knew had nothing at all to do with the attack on the consulate, would be brought to justice. How you do that to someone who has just lost a child, I do not know. Her mendacity is not really in dispute. It isn't just the people who oppose her who say she lies. Her supporters know it well too, and don't care, because they want the things that her lies are meant to secure for them. She is *their liar.*

But the past century has been awash in lies. We err if we assume that things were always so. The spirit might have been willing enough, but the technology was weak. A town crier simply cannot spread lies continually and from one end of a nation to the other. Mass education, what Muggeridge called the "great fraud and mumbo-jumbo of the age," can do it, as can mass media. It is what they are for, really. Muggeridge said that he was conscious of having been governed throughout his life by a long miserable series of buffoons and liars. The joke in the old Soviet Union was that there was no Pravda (Truth) in *Izvestia* (*The News*), and no Izvestia in *Pravda*. Is the *New York Times* much more honest? Walter Duranty, whom Muggeridge actually liked as a human being while calling him "the most accomplished liar I have ever met," helped to bolster Stalin's image by reporting that no, there was no starvation in the Ukraine and that the forced collectivization of farms was proceeding just fine. Was it five or six million people whom Stalin slew in the Ukraine? People were eating human corpses, it had gotten so bad, and what had been one of the richest areas in the world for the growing of grain was turned into a wilderness of weeds, idle machinery, and death. Duranty won the Pulitzer Prize for his reporting, a prize the Pulitzer Board has never withdrawn.

We now know, from the confessions of one of the fabricators (Dr. Bernard Nathanson) and the boasts of another (Dr. Alan Guttmacher) that the statistics upon which the Supreme Court based its infamous decision on abortion were just made up—for example, that a million American women had died from illegal abortions. How far wrong was that statistic? It is like saying that three decades ago the earth's temperature was five hundred degrees, or that a human skeleton had been discovered at another Piltdown, measuring a hundred feet in length. The lies have been amply documented. Has anyone other than the repentant Dr. Nathanson of blessed memory hung his head in shame and recanted? Or do any legal experts say, "It disgusts us to have to endure this decision, based as it was on sheer mendacity"? No, never. The lies are *our lies*. Harvey Milk was an openly homosexual politician in San Francisco, assassinated along with the mayor. His assassination had nothing to do with his sexual predilections. Mr. Milk was also a serial predator of teenage boys. That will get you a Hollywood movie and actual "religious" icons, featuring the man with a halo. They will name a street after you. They will produce daft picture books of Mr. Milk, dressed and not tumescent, for the consumption of little children in school. The lies are *our lies*.

Do we any longer have a sense of honor? What does it mean when we make a solemn promise? I know of several abandoned spouses—wives or husbands of adulterers—who have *lost custody of the children,* possibly because being abandoned by a lying and cheating lout or whore has the tendency to make you angry, and anger does not play well in court. How is this possible, unless we really no longer expect people to tell the truth and to abide by their promises? King Lear could cry out upon false judges who commit the very crimes for which they condemn others. We go farther than that. We have judges who commit the very crimes *for which they reward others.*

Here we encounter the weakling's objection. "You can't judge others," says the weakling, crooking his finger, or cocking her head knowingly, like an intelligent retriever, "because you don't know what you would do unless you were in the same situation. You don't know how trying it is." And then comes the list of unexpected evils and disappointments, and the dry handkerchief dabbing at the eyes. I make no boast about what I would or would not do. I insist instead, if I prove myself to be on the verge of breaking a solemn promise, that *other men hold me to it,* just as a corporal orders the recruit to remain at his station, and his buddies make sure he does. Nobody knows what the battlefield is like until the bullets fly and the grenades explode. That is precisely what vows are for. "I promise to be true so long as it is convenient to me" is not a promise at all. It is itself a lie—a mock promise.

Am I being too harsh here? Let us ask ourselves this simple question. When was the last time you heard someone admit to a lie without legal compulsion and without making excuses or attempting to shift the blame onto someone else? When was the last time you heard of someone's *conscience* compelling him to come clean? When was the last time you heard someone say, "I am going to break a promise, and break some hearts in doing so. Please pray for me, because I will need it, as I am entering with eyes wide open into the valley of the shadow of death. Naturally I will resign from all my positions of public influence and trust."

We must become tellers of truth again—and people who are willing to hear truths, too, especially when it hurts to hear them.

Clear Your Mind of Cant

Here is a first step.

One of the most powerful influences upon my thought when I was young was Joseph Boswell's *Life of Johnson.* If Samuel Johnson had been born in our time, he would have had the genius drugged out of him by the various pharmaceutical enemies of boyhood; he might be finger-painting with Einstein and Mozart in a group home or a reformatory. But in the eighteenth century his peculiar sensitivity and his many obsessions made him more human, not less; more apt to perceive the motives and the feelings of others, because he had been so accustomed to confronting the darkest and worst of his own self. Johnson was like a lone gladiator in the arena, said Boswell, standing up against the beasts when they came lunging from their cages.

One day Boswell expressed a wish to be in Parliament but noted, "Perhaps, sir, I should be the less happy for being in Parliament. I would never sell my vote, and I should be vexed if things went wrong." "That's cant, sir," replied Johnson. "It would not vex you more in the House than in the gallery: public affairs vex no man." He explained, "I have never slept an hour less, nor ate an ounce less meat" because of a vote in Parliament, and he urged his friend, "clear your *mind* of cant."

There is a form of cant that we call "small talk," useful in polite conversation. "You may *talk* as other people do," Johnson told Boswell, "you may say to a man, 'Sir, I am your most humble servant.' You are *not* his most humble servant.... You may *talk* in this manner; it a mode of talking in society: but don't *think* foolishly."

I believe now that the "higher cant" is too dangerous even for small talk, because we will inevitably end up thinking in its terms. Words like *democracy, diversity, equality, inclusivity, marginalization, misogyny, racism, sexism, homophobia, imperialism, colonialism, progressivism, autonomy,* and many others my readers might name are simply terms of political force and have no real meaning anymore. Some of them never had any meaning to begin with. Do not wash your food in chlorine. Do not sprinkle your thoughts with poison.

The cant is everywhere—on television, on the radio, in newspapers and magazines, on billboards, in advertisements of all kinds, in the doctor's office, in your school (very little else is in your school), in many a pulpit (alas), and on the lips of almost everybody you will meet.

This is not the common talk of ordinary people in ordinary times. When the fishermen on an old schooner set down for the night, they did not talk about *democracy, diversity, equality, inclusivity,* and the rest of the nonsense. They talked about their work: the sea, good spots for cod or halibut, the ropes, the bad food, sails that needed repair, what ports they had visited, and what they saw and did there. They talked about home, their children, the woman waiting for one of them in Saint John's, various misadventures with the police. They talked about human things. They might sing songs, or play cards or chess or checkers, or whittle scrimshaw. If one of them did launch into political cant, he'd be roared down by the others or have a shot of whiskey splashed in his face.

You have to be *educated into* cant; it is a kind of stupidity that surpasses the capacity of unaided Nature to confer. Mass phenomena do the job, so that when you see someone whose brains have been addled by cant for a long time, say a politician, it is as if you were watching a puppet flapping its mouth while a ventriloquist made it say *democracy, diversity, equality, inclusivity*; you might provide the words yourself if you were in a mischievous mood. Try it someday. When you find a canting politician or journalist or commentator on television, turn off the sound and supply the words. There is no mind there, only a predictable drone of empty words where a mind used to be.

Here is a quick and generally reliable rule to follow. If people have always said it, it is probably true; it is the distilled wisdom of the ages. If people have not always said it, but everybody is saying it *now,* it is probably a lie; it is the concentrated madness of the moment.

People are especially prone to cant when they describe their feelings in public. When someone says, "I am offended by that remark," the first thing you must think, in our time, is that the remark has broken upon the person's day like the bright sun through a week of rain and gloom. An owl is not offended by the little field mouse; it is just what the owl is on the lookout for. If the offended person loses any sleep that night, it will not be for sorrow, but for delightful dreams of vengeance and public displays of virtue. The cannibal rolls up his sleeves and whets the knife. For truly tolerant people are hard to offend. They do not seek occasion to bring others into ill repute. They do not put the worst construction on someone else's words or deeds.

When someone says, "I am truly saddened by the words of my political opponent," or philosophical opponent, or theological opponent, or whatever, it is almost always a lie. A chess player is not *saddened* when his opponent plunks his queen down in just the place for a deadly fork. He can hardly believe his eyes. So it was that Joab, catching Abner with his guard down, took him aside for a nice chat, and that was the end of Abner (2 Samuel 3: 23–27).

Nature and Vacuums

The lie rushes in to fill up the void left by truth in retreat. When people lose their faith in God, for example, they do not then believe in nothing. It is as Chesterton said. They commence believing in *anything,* usually the nearest and biggest thing, the gross power of the state to solve all human problems. Or they begin to worship their own most powerful physical and emotional drives. Or they worship what they *wish* would be the biggest thing in the world, themselves. Self, sex, and the state, the three most obvious substitutes, or the three together, the three-poisoned god. All you need to do to determine what a people worship is to look at their parades. For us in the West now, the parade isn't a procession on the feast of Corpus Christi, with everyone in the village lining the streets to pray and sing *Pange, lingua, gloriosi* as the priest passes by with the Sacrament. I do not need to mention what our parade now is, who the priests are, what they celebrate, what language they use, how they are robed (or disrobed), what they ingest, and what brings so many people to watch.

The point here is that the lie cannot be defeated by a vacuity. It has to be defeated by truth. But since we are embodied souls, the truth we are seeking must not be merely abstract. An ax cannot compete against a Sherman tank, unless the Sherman tank is an abstract tank, an idea of a tank; the ax can smash that sort of tank all the time. Therefore we have to immerse ourselves in *things*: trees, stars, mud, grouse, hay, stones, brooks, rain, dogs, fire; and the manmade things closest to the human hand and its work: hammer, shovel, paintbrush, wrench, wheel. The poet Gerard Manley Hopkins is my inspiration here:

> Glory be to God for dappled things,
> For skies of couple-color as a brinded cow;
> For rose-moles all in stipple upon trout that swim,
> Fresh fire-coal chestnut-falls, finches' wings,
> Landscape plotted and pieced, fold, fallow, and plough,
> And all trades, their gear and tackle and trim.

It is hard to go completely mad if you spend your free time being free and accepting the free bounties of the world round about. Consider the conversation of human beings before the advent of mass media. A boy could grow up and never see anything obscene at all; where would it come from? Something puerile scrawled on the side of an outhouse? Meanwhile, the boy would roam the village or the woods and learn things, learn about *things,* every day. I have been reading the letters of Dr. Horatio Robinson Storer, who was the leader of the movement for the reform of abortion laws in nineteenth-century America. He wanted to bring those laws into harmony with scientific discoveries and with the clear moral law. Of course, at that time it meant that since the embryo was obviously alive and human in genus and species, an independent self-organizing entity needing the mother for shelter and nourishment but not a biological part of the mother or an inert thing inside her, the law and social customs would have to respect the *fact*. No slogans allowed. Abortion was plainly the killing of a human being.

In any case, the Storers sent their boy Horatio off to a boarding school on Cape Cod, and when he wasn't studying Latin and arithmetic, he and the other boys combed the shores, miles and miles of them, in all kinds of weather. They went fishing, hunting for crabs, checking up on a shark skeleton that had washed up, calling on a local naturalist, identifying and collecting birds' eggs, hunting pheasant, and building a fortress. Think of how much *reality* they stuffed into their heads while they stuffed their pockets with shells!

I can illustrate with a series of questions. You are on a beach on Cape Cod. The wind is coming from the southwest. What does that mean? How can you tell that it is the southwest and not the southeast when you don't have a compass? The tide is in. How can you tell that? Tomorrow there will be a full moon. How do you know that? What does that have to do with the tide? Where are you likely to find clams? Will it be better in about twelve hours, when the tide is out? How do you know that? You want to loaf about the shore in a canoe. The canoe is leaking a little. What can you use to stop up the leak? Where can you find it?

The man in the house on the point has been catching eels. How do you do that? Where are you likely to find them? What bait do you use? When you catch one (young Storer reported having seen one three feet long), how do you cook it? Next week you want to go somewhere that is ten miles away rather than five, so you won't be able to walk there; you'll have to take a horse or mule. What's the difference in how they ride? How do you curry a horse when you bring him in for the night? There's a male horse in the stables named Joey. What did they have to do to him to make him tame enough for children? When would you do that? How would you keep him from bleeding to death?

How do you butcher a pig? How do you build a smokehouse for the bacon? What kind of wood do you use for the fire, and why? How thick should you cut the flitches of the bacon? Where would you find the wood? How can you tell a maple from an oak? What can you do with quince, angelica root, sassafras, chokecherries, bilberries, hazelnuts, beechnuts, birch bark, willow bark, and the resin from pine trees? How do you tap a maple tree for syrup?

How do you graft sweet apples on a hardier trunk? How do you keep a beehive? What does the honeycomb taste like? When do you gather cranberries? Are they still good if they are on the ground the next spring? What are those birds that descend upon berry bushes in big flocks, nibbling the berries and passing them along to one another? What is the bird they call a yellowhammer? When do the warblers pass through on their way north or south?

How do you clear trees and stumps from a field? How do you handle a mattock? What is an ice saw? How do you know if the ice on a pond is thick enough for skating? How do you cut blocks of ice for use in the summer? How do you keep them from melting? What do you do with the eyes of potatoes if you want to plant them? How do you make sour-dough bread? Is that mushroom growing out of the side of a tree, looking like a beefsteak, good to eat?

What is that bright red star in the night sky that does not keep the same place among the constellations? If you wanted to find Jupiter in the sky, where would you generally look? Why, on Cape Cod, is the sun never directly over your head? What makes the days so short in winter? If you want to make bricks, where would you be likely to find a good clay pit? What kind of stone is marble? What is soapstone, feldspar, mica, obsidian, jasper?

I have asked my freshman honors students at college where in the sky the sun will be, in the middle of the afternoon in September, here in Rhode Island. They don't know. They are strangers to the world, but they certainly are *not* strangers to the lies and folly that are the stock in trade, as I have said, of mass entertainment, mass education, and mass politics.

Things, in their beautiful and imposing integrity, do not easily bend to lies. A bull is a bull and not a cow. Grass is food for cattle but not for man. A warbler is alive but a rock is not. The three-hundred-pound stone will not move for a little child or a boy or a feminist professor. Water expands when it freezes and will break anything unless you allow for that. Things are what they are. They know no slogans, and they do not lie.

And they give witness to the glory of God.

Learn to Speak and Read

Imagine someone with a peculiar visual handicap. He is not color blind, exactly. He can see the three primary colors and the three secondary colors. He can see red (he often sees red), orange, yellow, green, blue, and purple. We'll give him also white and black and brown. But that is *all* he can see. He has no other words for color. If you asked him to describe the color of a fox, he would say it was red, red like an apple.

Such a person would be completely incapable of appreciating a painting by the Little Dyer, the affectionate nickname the Italians gave to Jacopo Robusti: *Tintoretto*. He would see blocks of the elementary colors on a billboard, but he could make nothing of the bright burst of a white kind of gold over the head of Christ as he leans over like a priest to give the holy bread to the apostle nearest to him, in Tintoretto's "Last Supper." His eyes would register the light, but his mind would not see its qualities.

He would be like the people in Orwell's *1984*, who are to be rendered incapable of rebellion because they would be incapable of independent thought. And they would be incapable of independent thought because of the deliberate obliteration of real English, to be replaced by Newspeak, with all shades of meaning reduced to simple negatives and simple amplifiers. What do we need all those words for, anyway, says Syme, the linguist, to Winston Smith? Why should we have words like *fine, splendid, excellent*, and the rest, when *good, plus-good,* and *double-plus-good* will do?

Syme is a nihilist with a passion about linguistic destruction that borders on the religious. Smith says to himself that Syme knows too much, and that will prove dangerous to him. Sure enough, there comes a day when Syme no longer shows up for work.

If our language is inane and empty, our thoughts will be inane and empty too. Garbage in, garbage out. My students write badly not because teachers in high school never made them write papers. They have written plenty of papers—far too many, in fact. They have absorbed the Newspeak and cannot rid themselves of it. They do not need to learn a second language. They need to learn their own language, in all its richness. The

only way to do that is to read good books, books written before the current rage of Newspeak.

Let me give an example of what English was. I am not choosing it
because of the renown of the author or the work. In fact, I am choosing
it because the work is *not even meant to be great*. It is meant to be ordinary. The passage describes a stage in the career of the Renaissance
painter Filippino Lippi:

> At Rome the antique inspired him, not as an historian, a
> humanist, or a scholar, but as a painter and a poet who dis-
> covered in it new elements of delight. The antique appeared
> to him as an inexhaustible source of the picturesque: the rich
> ornamentation with its foliage, garlands, masks, trophies, was
> like a new toy in his hands. He even enriched it still more with
> whatever he could find of Oriental luxury—Moorish, Chi-
> nese. "It is marvelous," writes Vasari, "to see the strange
> fancies which he has expressed in his painting. He was always
> introducing vases, foot-gear, temple-ornaments, head-dresses,
> strange trappings, armor, trophies, scimitars, swords, togas,
> cloaks, and an array of things so various and so beautiful that
> we owe him today a great and eternal obligation for all the
> beauty and ornamentation that he thus added to our art."

That passage could not be written now. The language is too immersed
in *things,* the specific objects of interest and beauty which Filippino Lippi
gazed upon and studied, as a child in a curiosity shop, where everything
fascinates, because it is "original, counter, spare, strange," to use Hopkins's happy line. But the passage is also too sensitive to the spiritual state
of Lippi's very being. The painter is not labeled and tagged for his politics,
or for his technical achievements, or for his progress as a careerist, or for
his supposedly unorthodox or "transgressive" depictions, or for the
seamy side of his personal life—about the only things that would interest
the academic world now. The author is trying to reveal to us something
of the man himself, which also is something of the image of God within

him. His article ends with words whose delicacy and precision are really meant to present the artist in full to our imagination: "Of the generation immediately preceding the great works of Michelangelo and Leonardo, of that restless and subtle, complex and nervous generation of Botticelli and Cosimo Rosselli, he is perhaps the most varied, the most gifted, and the most lovable."

Those words were not written in a book of art history. They were written by the art historian Louis Gillet for the *Catholic Encyclopedia*, published in 1910, a more than ten-thousand-page compendium of learning and instruction. What should impress us is not just the breadth of knowledge that Gillet takes for granted in his readers—that they will know who George Vasari was, and to what "Oriental luxury" might refer, and at what time Michelangelo and Leonardo da Vinci were at the peak of their powers as painters. True, the article presupposes this *information,* to use the dead modern word. But there is other than information. Gillet takes for granted that the reader can be touched at the core of his humanity: that it will matter to him that Filippino Lippi was "a poet," that is, a maker, one who sees wisely into the truth of things and their hidden relations with one another, into the power they possess to reveal the truth to us, if we wait upon them in silence and humility. The encyclopedia depends not just on what the reader is expected to *know*, but on what the reader is expected to *be*.

To be more specific, Monsieur Gillet expects that his readers have souls for poetry. That was not considered the enclave of the rich or of long-haired bohemians starving in their Parisian garret. Every single culture known to man—*except for ours*—has its poetry, not as the livelihood of "creative writers" ensconced in institutions of higher learning, because otherwise they would have to live under bridges and filch fruit from outdoor stands, but as the common heritage of the people. Before there was even an alphabet there were songs, and a child's first experience of poetry was to *hear it* sung, in the lays of the gods and of ancient kings and warriors. The Greek lad heard the rhapsode sing of the rage of Achilles that sent the souls of many fine men to Hades and left their bodies strewn on the earth to be a feast for birds and dogs. The Saxon lad heard

the *scop* sing of the loyal friendship of Sigemund and his nephew Fitela
and how they slew the dragon and recovered the treasure. The French
lad heard the troubadour sing the old song of Roland and Oliver, and
how they died at Roncesvalles defending the pass for Charlemagne
against the Saracens.

We have no songs in our memories. Every human culture before ours
has raised up poetry as the noblest of the human arts. The Psalms are
poems, Job is one of the most sublime poems ever composed, and there
is nothing in the ancient world that is quite like the consoling and hope-
filled poetry of the prophet Isaiah. Poetry is not for students at the university. It is for everyone. I do not mean the acutely self-conscious or
snobbishly academic or crassly sexual stuff that passes for poetry now,
the interest of a few specialists and of mutually admiring or envious poets
themselves. I especially do not mean the poetry without music that goes
by the name of "free verse," almost all of which is very poor, and none
of which can ever really enter the memory. I mean the great tradition,
the poems that bring people of all ages together, poems that range from
the sublime to the simple; from Milton's *Paradise Lost* to Longfellow's
Song of Hiawatha, lyrics by Keats, dramatic monologues by Robert
Browning, the deeply sane flights of fancy by Coleridge—everything that
ordinary people once loved. And make no mistake: they were ordinary
people. Laura Ingalls Wilder recalled receiving a much-treasured gift for
her sixteenth birthday out on the prairies of South Dakota. It was a
volume of poetry by Lord Tennyson. My college freshmen now do not
even know who Tennyson was.

"Load every rift with ore," said Keats, describing what a true poet
must do; no stanza, no line is to remain dull and blank and merely func-
tional. What Keats did with poems, we ought to do with our minds,
claiming for our own the gold that the poets give us. Load every rift of
the mind with ore. Let the poets teach us how to read and speak and
think.

What difference will that make? Let us see. A couple of academic
ethicists in Italy say that, since abortion is perfectly all right, and since
there is no real difference between a newborn baby and the fetus in the

womb, infanticide ought to be legal up to some arbitrary age. And I hear in my mind's ear the warning of the Duke of Albany to his evil and ambitious wife, Goneril, who has plotted against her own aged and helpless father, King Lear. If such unnatural deeds are to be permitted, he says, "Humanity must perforce prey on itself / Like monsters of the deep." *That* clears the mind. Or you hear a woman anxious to make sure that her four-year-old child gets into the "best" preschool because she has Harvard in her mind; but your mind turns to Robert Frost, a poet and farmer and teacher who worked hard all his life, and Frost reminds you that the heart of life is something other than work: "One could do worse than be a swinger of birches." Or you stumble upon an atheist casting foolish and bigoted contempt upon believers, when he knows neither what they believe nor why, and the fine couplets of Alexander Pope ring in your mind:

> A little learning is a dangerous thing:
> Drink deep, or taste not that Pierian spring,
> For one short draught intoxicates the brain,
> But drinking largely sobers us again.

We want not plastic coins but gold. Fill your heart and mind with it. If you knew there was a beach where you could pick up gold nuggets like pebble stones, would you not go there? Go there.

TWO

EXCEPT THE LORD BUILD THE HOUSE:
Restoring a Sense of Beauty

John Senior, whose book *The Restoration of Christian Culture* is a late inspiration of mine, records the thoughts of Henry Adams when he went with his friend the scientist Samuel Pierpont Langley to see the Great Exposition in Paris in 1900. Langley wanted nothing better than to show off one form of engine after another: the dynamo, the thing that turns and transfers mechanical energy or creates electrical energy for other use. Assuredly I would not be able to type these words on a computer if it were not for things that are made to turn, by wind or water or the burning of coal or oil or the heat released in the fission of radioactive atoms. I would be writing them with a pen, on paper.

Adams found it impressive and inhuman, and finally he escaped in his imagination to the cathedral of Our Lady of Chartres. The men who built Europe's greatest Gothic church did not have diesel engines, or lightweight metals like soft aluminum or firm titanium, or steel girders. They did not have cranes that could tower a hundred feet in the air without toppling, while lifting pre-formed blocks of concrete. They did not have computer models. They did not have the calculus. Most of them assuredly could not read. They had to fit stones atop one another precisely to be both balanced and beautiful, and that meant that the stones had to be cleanly and accurately dressed, shaved with saws, cut to fit. Their carpenters had to know how to build safe scaffolding from the hewn trunks of hardwood trees, to soar ten or twelve stories in the air, supporting the men who, with sledges and pulleys and main strength, set in place the stones of lovely arches, springing on each side at exactly the same oblique angle from the pillars beneath, to intersect one another at a point clinched by the keystone.

It is not enough to say that Chartres Cathedral is a great work of art. A sketch by Rembrandt is a great work of art. A single rib of a single pillar at Chartres is a great work of craftsmanship. A single panel of one of the lesser stained glass windows along the nave gives us art at its finest. Chartres is a magnificent symphony of countless works of sculpture, glazing, tiling, carpentry, masonry—and poetry and theology too. It is more than a museum or a collection. In a museum, one work is displayed next to another because it happens to have been created by the same person or in the same country or at around the same time. But every work in Chartres has to do with every other. I would say that there is nothing like it in the world, except that in fact there are things like it—all the other great cathedrals of the Middle Ages are like it, all over Europe; and thousands of churches, too, some of them the special churches for orders of priests, like Santa Maria Novella, the Dominican church in Florence, and some of them just the principal church for a small town or a village, which would give you a kind of Chartres in miniature. At the Great Exposition, every entry boasted an inventor, but if you visit many an old church in Europe, you will see frescoes or sculptures created by "the Master of Anytown," whose name no one knows.

We still cannot reproduce the deep rich blue of the windows of Chartres. But it is not my point here to compare medieval art favorably with modern art. It is to notice what it is that people believe to be most important in our common life on earth. If you went to the Great Exposition, you might suppose that the most important thing is to make machines that turn things, so as to work other machines, to do things we want them to do, or to make things we want them to make. If you went to Chartres, you would not need to suppose, you would simply and readily perceive that the most important thing was to sing with the Psalmist, "I rejoiced when I heard them say, Let us go up to the house of the Lord."

Drab, the Enemy

In C. S. Lewis's fantastical novel *That Hideous Strength*, when the planet-traveler Ransom prepares to greet old Merlin the mage from Arthurian times, he dons a long red and gold robe. That surprises his friends, but he reminds them that in all other times but our own, "drab was not a favorite color."

Drab is a favorite color in our day; its companion is garish. I defy any of my contemporaries to name one style of public building or style of dress or form of popular entertainment that is not now either drab or garish. Our churchmen, no better educated than anyone else in the humanities and the Christian heritage of art, architecture, and music, have gone along with the movement, mostly drab, but sometimes garish, as witness the big childish banners blaring out a favorite comforting verse (never "It is a terrible thing to fall into the hands of the living God"), the glad-handing ceremonies of greeting and peace-wishing, the rock bands in the sanctuary, big screens like stadium scoreboards to flash the mantras of the songs, and the smiling Protestant minister in jeans, or the Catholic priest with a jowly smile, far more comfortable joshing with the attendees than praying with people who are, as he is, as we all are, on the inevitable journey to the grave and in dire need of the grace of God.

When my daughter and I were in Sweden, we stopped in many a rural church built during the Middle Ages and then subjected to artistic reforms afterward. Sometimes I saw shadows that looked like water stains emerging through the plaster of the ceilings. I began to suspect that they were not stains or tricks of the light. When I asked a conservative minister about them, he confirmed my suspicion. Many fresco paintings were whitewashed away in the so-called Enlightenment; it was that same Enlightenment, in its sanguinary French eruption, that smashed priceless stained glass windows in churches and cathedrals across the country. "Four fifths of [man's] greatest art," said Henry Adams, was created in those supposedly dark days, to the honor of Jesus and Mary. The Enlightenment destroyed more great art than it produced, and what the harbingers of the *novus ordo saeclorum* did not get around to destroying they slandered.

There was, however, a generally healthy revival of Gothic art and architecture in the nineteenth century, thanks to the efforts of men like A. W. N. Pugin and John Ruskin; and when Catholics immigrated to the United States from Italy, France, Germany, Ireland, and Portugal, they did not aim to build trapezoidal meeting houses with clear windows and no representations of the history of salvation. They aimed to build *churches,* and they achieved that aim. I have seen an inscription on the facade of a Portuguese church in New Bedford reading, in Latin, "The workmen of Saint Anthony's built this to the glory of God." I do not think that the inscription implied that they only paid for the construction. They did hire a master builder, but the men did the work—with their hands, their sweat, at risk of life and limb. And these were not rich industrialists but fishermen. In my home town the church-builders were Irish coal miners, and they built their Saint Thomas Aquinas Church in Romanesque style, pooling their funds to hire an Italian painter who had done some work on the rotunda of the Capitol in Washington. He came to lowly Archbald, Pennsylvania, and filled the church with paintings, nave and sanctuary, walls and ceiling. My boyhood church was beautiful. Then came the rage for the drab and the garish, and a good deal of that original beauty was obliterated, spoiled, or pulverized—at considerable expense.

Drab, with garish its cousin, is our enemy. Think of it. It is a truth as plain and embarrassing as a dead fish rotting and stinking in the sun. Does anyone go to visit the modern neighborhoods of Rome, built in drab? Does anyone take pictures of a new police station or a new post office? The most prominent features of the new county courthouse where

we live are enormous glass "walls," so that you can see into empty waiting rooms and hallways, and a sheltered area surmounted with a big
metal fence and rolls of barbed wire.

Our young people are not only starved for nature. They are starved
for beauty. Everywhere they turn, their eyes fall upon what is drab or
garish: their schools, their music, new books for sale, the fast-food joint,
a baseball stadium (where you can hardly talk to the fan sitting next to
you, for the noise roaring out at you from the loudspeakers), and, of
course, their churches. Saint Paul wanted to be all things to all men, to
save some (1 Corinthians 9:22). We have applied his dictum to what
surrounds us. We are drab with the drab, garish with the garish, inane
with the inane, and we save nobody at all.

Rip Out the Plywood

I have seen, in Catholic churches, minimalist Stations of the Cross
that cannot even be recognized if you are more than a few feet away. The
message they deliver is that the Stations are trivial. I have seen crosses
that look as if a modernist Jesus were flying with wings outspread, like
a theological pterodactyl. The message is that the cross was a brief and
unfortunate interlude. I have heard tunes that would not be acceptable
for a jingle to sell jelly doughnuts on television. The message is that religion is childish and is something offered up for our consumption, if we
have a taste for that sort of thing. I have seen the Sacrament relegated to
what looks like a broom closet. The message is that it is something to be
embarrassed about and that we come to church not to serve God but to
celebrate our own central goodness. I have seen one sculpture of the
supper at Emmaus that has Jesus at one end of the table with the two
disciples and two other figures ten or twelve feet away; it looks as if they
are arguing with one another, perhaps dickering over the check for the
meal. If you were not told that it was the supper at Emmaus, there is no
way you could guess it. There is no message but chaos. I have seen a
baptismal font with bubbles. The message is that flashy technology is to
be preferred before silence. I have seen beautifully tiled floors, their

intricate cruciform patterns bespeaking careful and devoted craftsmanship, covered over with a plush red carpet, wall to wall, such as might
be used in a whorehouse down on its luck. The message is that we are
the newly rich, with bad taste. I have heard for decades effeminate
"hymns" with the structure and melody of off-Broadway show tunes.
The message is that boys should outgrow religion when they start to
shave, and that girls should eventually follow their lead—as they do. I
have seen hymn texts altered so as to obliterate references to God with
the personal pronoun "He." The message is that God is not personal at
all but a concept, a thing.

It is long past the time to get rid of everything ugly and stupid from
our churches, most of it visited upon them since the great iconoclasm of
the sixties, and return to genuine art, art that stirs the imagination and
pleases the eye, that entices the soul with beauty—even sometimes a
dread beauty—before a single word of a sermon is uttered.

Let me use an analogy here. I am involved in the restoration of an
old home that for more than a hundred years served as the rectory of a
Catholic parish in Nova Scotia. One of the first things we did was to tear
out wall-to-wall carpeting that had gotten dingy and moldy over the
years. Beneath the carpeting lay plywood. In the kitchen it was the same
thing, except it was not carpet we pulled up but linoleum. What lay
underneath the plywood and linoleum? Would it be the old sub-floor,
with rough-hewn timbers?

No, not the sub-floor. What we found in most of the rooms were
oak and maple floors, with three-inch wide strips laid in handsome patterns, squares enclosing diagonals, and a large diamond set in the center
of the original parlor. The craftsmanship was impressive, the execution
precise. Those floors alone would now command the price of an entire
house. The other floors showed less of the fine arts but more of history
and the power of nature: large planks of seasoned hemlock, which
absorbs moisture from the air and grows tougher from it. The hemlock
was the flooring for the original house—as old as the foundation itself.

In our houses we have recovered from the rage to paste plywood and
paneling over hardwood floors and plaster walls. In that one regard we

now shake our heads in dismay over the Decades that Taste Forgot. What we do not yet see is that the plywood is in a hundred other places too: in schools, social customs, dress, eateries, reading habits, entertainment, sports, music, and art. The plywood is not just in the rectory. It is in the church. And you are not just walking on it. You are looking at plywood on the walls, hearing plywood from the pulpit, and singing plywood instead of hymns.

Time to rip out the plywood.

If Music Be the Food of Love

What to do first? It takes many years for someone to learn how to play a musical instrument well, and the organ, the king of instruments, is not for someone who can jitter about on a keyboard. Of course we need organists, but before we can have them in any number, we can use the musical instrument wherein everyone is at least somewhat proficient: the human voice. *We can sing.*

We have a treasury of excellent hymns, lying in a chest in an attic. Bring them down. This is not a matter of prescribing one style for everyone. There are two reasons why. The first is that those hymns we no longer sing represent a wonderful variety of styles already. There are the straightforward American revival hymns ("Jesus, Keep Me Near the Cross"). There are haunting Irish folk melodies (the tune "Slane" for "Be Thou My Vision"). There are the poignant Negro spirituals ("There Is a Balm in Gilead"). We have medieval plainsong, featuring some of the oldest extant melodies ("Creator of the Stars of Night"); harmonizations of Renaissance melodies by Johann Sebastian Bach ("Jesus, Priceless Treasure"); melodies specifically written for fine religious lyrics ("Lux Benigna" for Cardinal Newman's "Lead, Kindly Light"); lilting melodies from the Scottish tradition ("Saint Columba," "Crimond," and "Evan" for "The King of Love My Shepherd Is"); the powerful shape-note hymns from Appalachia; French carols; English anthems for the Church militant; texts whose authors range from the Church Fathers to the pious blind poet Fanny Crosby;

melodies from the time of Ambrose to the beginning of the twentieth century, from every single nation in Europe. If someone rejects *all of that,* it is not because he does not appreciate "the" style. It is because he has a lust for destructiveness or because he does in fact want *one style* to prevail, the style of the jingling show tune, a style that has no place in the liturgy.

Some church choirs with a chokehold on the music protest that it takes them many long hours to learn a new hymn. That would be true only if they were singing in harmony, and most do not. It should take only a few minutes for anybody, in the choir or not, to learn to sing a new melody. The old hymns were written precisely for congregational singing. You do not have to be Beverly Sills or Mario Lanza to sing them. They are waiting; just as if there were a great wing of a castle that no one ever entered anymore, filled with works of art by the masters. No doubt a painting of the Prodigal Son by Murillo or Rembrandt reveals its secrets only gradually, so that you can look at it for the fiftieth time and notice something you had never noticed before, or wonder about something that you had seen but taken for granted, such as why Rembrandt's prodigal has a shaved head, or why there is a little white dog in mid-leap after Murillo's prodigal, wagging his tail for joy. But those great works also appeal to us immediately, impressing us with their beauty and suggesting that there always will be more, and more, to see and to learn and to delight in. The great hymns are like the paintings in that way. They give us riches at the outset and yet have more and more to give, in abundance.

Let some examples suffice. Here is "The King of Love My Shepherd Is," one of the many English settings of the beloved Psalm 23. Each stanza renders into English and Christian poetry one or two of the verses of the Hebrew original. How do you do that? By seeing all things in the enlightening glory of Christ. Take these verses: "Yea, though I walk through the valley of the shadow of death, I shall fear no evil, for Thou art with me; Thy rod and Thy staff, they comfort me." In the hands of a poet who knows what he is doing, they are raised to the summit of Calvary:

In death's dark vale I fear no ill,
With thee, dear Lord, beside me;
Thy rod and staff my comfort still,
Thy cross before to guide me.

There, without any fanfare, without the obvious word-thrashing of a would-be religious poet longing to show off what he learned in his graduate school course in Christology, the poet simply and quietly gives us a new way to look at what it means to be led by the Good Shepherd and his crozier. It is good to have the Lord keep suffering away from you, as you walk through the fearful valley. It is better for the Lord to transform your suffering into redemption, as you join him confidently upon the hill of crucifixion. Then you can say with the splendid and brave poet of "Jesu, meine Freude":

Fires may flash,
And thunders crash,
Yea, and death and hell assail me;
Jesus will not fail me.

Contemporary "hymns" exist in a make-believe safe space, like the blanket a child hangs over a couple of chairs to pretend that he is in a different world where monsters and big brothers cannot get at him. Yet I give them too much credit, because they are not so imaginative as that, and there is nothing really childlike about them. Children do not celebrate themselves, as contemporary Catholic and liberal Protestant hymns encourage us to do; they are too caught up in wonder at things like the sky and grass and mighty oak trees and frogs. The old hymns tell the truth about us. We do sin, we are walking in roundabout routes but always downhill towards the grave, and we very sorely require the grace of God, or we shall be lost. How do you express these things without reducing them to a pious formula?

The old poets could do it. They could embed their thoughts and prayers in a dramatic scene taken from Scripture, turning it in a surprising direction. So the author of "Abide with Me" asks us to think of the time when the risen Lord was walking with the two disciples on their way to Emmaus. They did not recognize Him as He explained the Scriptures to them, showing them that the Christ had to suffer and die to redeem the people and rise again on the third day. Their hearts burned within them. They did not want the conversation to end, so when they approached an inn, they said to Him, "Tarry with us yet awhile, Lord, for the evening draws near." *That* is the inspiration for the poet. Here are the first two verses:

> Abide with me; fast falls the eventide;
> The darkness deepens; Lord, with me abide.
> When other helpers fail and comforts flee,
> Help of the helpless, O abide with me.
> Swift to its close ebbs out life's little day;
> Earth's joys grow dim, its glory flies away;
> Change and decay in all around I see:
> O thou who changest not, abide with me.

Those are lines that can take up abode in the heart as long as you live. The way to Emmaus is the way to old age and death, but if the Lord will tarry, if the Lord will abide within us and make His dwelling place there, if He will be the broken bread for the evening meal, then we have nothing to fear:

> Hold thou thy cross before my closing eyes;
> Shine through the gloom, and point me to the skies;
> Heav'n's morning breaks, and earth's vain shadows flee:
> In life, in death, O Lord, abide with me.

Sing the hymns, then. That can be done *immediately*. A caveat, though. Many of the publishers of hymnals, sensing a certain disgruntlement among priests and their congregations, have included some "traditional" hymns to make their publications more excusable—more likely to be adopted by orthodox priests, as a fair compromise between the old and the new. Do not fall for the ruse.

First, there are some compromises we should never make. We should never compromise between beauty and slovenliness, between genuine poetry (however workmanlike it may be) and silly doggerel, and between orthodoxy and heresy. There is no reason to sing the contemporary jingles at all, and that will dispense with at least three quarters of the songs included in such bad hymnals as *Gather, Glory and Praise*, and the latest editions of *Worship* in the United States and Canada. But more important, *the texts* of the old hymns in those hymnals have been emasculated, so that you are not getting what the poets wrote. In only one trivial case that I know of ("There Is a Green Hill Far Away") has a text been recently emended for clarity. In all other cases, the emendations mess up the poetry because we are supposed to be allergic to the useful pronouns "thee" and "thine," or they remove masculine references to God, because we are smarter than the Lord who instructed us to call God "Father," or they obscure the unity of man that in English can only be rendered at once personal, singular, and universal by the word *man*, or they weaken the sense of the transcendence and the omnipotence of God, or they expunge references to the Church militant, or they soften a poet's frank admission of wretchedness and sin. It is as if someone were to paint a big grin on the face of the Mona Lisa, lest we be made too uncomfortable by her mysterious countenance. A stallion that is fixed is a stallion no more. Saint Paul urged the brothers at Corinth to acquit themselves like men—not like geldings.

Sing the old hymns. If poets want to compose new hymns, let them learn humbly from the old, because that is the only way to learn an art. What was necessary for Johann Sebastian Bach surely is not dispensable for the rest of us. While we are waiting for them to learn the art, and that may take a generation or two, we sing the old hymns, as I say. That's to begin. If we do that alone, it will be a very great deal.

There might be more. A glance at any sculpted choir in a medieval or Renaissance church will show us something that could again be done because it was done for many centuries. Those choirs feature choirboys.

They did not sing in unison. They did not sing in the fine four-part harmony for which all Protestant hymnals are scored and which any congregation, with practice and good cheer, can master. What was done before and everywhere in Christendom can be done again. The boys sang in polyphony, which came to its full flowering in the soaring choral compositions of Palestrina, Victoria, and Bach. Ralph Vaughan Williams, John Stainer, and John Tavener have shown us that sacred polyphony of the highest quality can still be composed, and there are still choirs in Europe, here and there, that feature the boy trebles for which those works were written, along with the mature male voices in alto, tenor, and bass. The only remaining choir school for boys in the United States, Saint Paul's in Cambridge, Massachusetts, performs music meant for transcendence; and, once upon a time, it was meant for everyone at one of thousands of large churches all over Europe.

I do not insist upon Palestrina and boy choirs. I do want to suggest, though, that we have an extraordinary form of art that the Church fostered and that was not beyond the capacity of ordinary people to execute and to enjoy. And we have advantages that our forebears did not have. The sheet music is easy to find; so are good performances to listen to. What they did then, we can do now.

Then there is Gregorian chant, the music the Church created specifically for prayer. It is not old-fashioned, but timeless; it involves the subtle adjustment of melody and voice to the meaning of the words sung and the occasion for singing them. It is not difficult to learn; it could not be, as it was meant to be sung by people without any special musical training. Its range of notes is comfortably within that of any one voice. Its intervals are almost always small, and when they are not, they are the easiest intervals to hear and to sing: the dominant (C to G) or subdominant (C to F). Notes are almost always of one beat or two. You never have the unnatural intervals and syncopation of the show tunes. You never begin, as the musically dreadful "On Eagle's Wings" does, on the major seventh. The idea is not to show off the virtuosity of a soloist auditioning for a part in *South Pacific* but to have the singers immerse themselves with ease into the melody and the meaning.

It is a mark of what we have lost that when I mention Gregorian chant, Catholics will think of the few stark and simple chants they still occasionally sing: the *Sanctus* and *Agnus Dei* from the old Mass for the Dead. Then they assume that all the rest of the chants are like chants for a funeral. Nothing could be farther from the truth. I am looking now at a *Paroissien romain*, a French Canadian book specifying the chants for every feast in the Church year, every special purpose for which a Mass may be said, and all the canonical hours. It is sixteen hundred pages long. The chant for the gradual for the Mass of matrimony renders in musical form this verse from Psalm 127 (Vulgate): *Uxor tua sicut vitis abundans in lateribus domus tuae; filii tui sicut novellae olivarum in circuitu mensae tuae.* "May your wife be like a fruitful vine in the recesses of your house; your children like olive shoots around your table." The chant is utterly joyful, ranging well into the higher regions of the scale. For those forty-three Latin syllables, the chant gives 255 notes, by my counting. Gregorian chant is leisurely in the truest sense: we assume in it that we are not compelled by time or stanzaic structure to end at any certain point, but rather are led by the meaning itself. It is horizontal and open-ended in its musical form, but vertical and transcendent in its clearing a space for meditation upon the words and the works of God.

My *Paroissien romain* was published in 1956, well within living memory. I took my copy from the closet of a choir loft. It was one among many that had sat there for years, unused. The church where I found it was no cathedral, no university chapel, but an ordinary parish church on an island inhabited by old French families in the fishing trade. What fishermen sang once, we can sing again.

Jesus, Priceless Treasure

"Where your treasure is," says Jesus, "there will your heart lie also." We can tell where a people's heart lies by where they place their treasure.

In material terms we are by far the wealthiest generation of people who have ever lived on earth. Yet our original accomplishments in all of the arts are meager at best. At worst, we show a heavy net deficit. The modern world has destroyed almost as many *forms of art*—not just individual works of art, but the very genres—as the people of the Middle Ages and the Renaissance invented. Renaissance painting and sculpture, music and poetry, are what you get when a vigorous popular and learned tradition that had already been immensely creative meets again the classics of Greece and Rome. Modern art is what you get when you repudiate the people, the tradition, and the classics. Individuals are left to trade upon the stock of their native creativity alone, which is not going to be great.

But we do spend money on buildings for mass entertainment. Cash-strapped cities are bullied by the owners of baseball and football teams to float bond issues for state-of-the-art stadiums, with computer-run scoreboards for flashing replays and commercials, booming sound-systems that batter the ears of fifty thousand people, food courts more varied and plentiful than a bazaar in old Baghdad in the days of the sultans, special enclaves where you can eat and drink without sparing while watching the ballgame through Plexiglass windows, grounds composed of special hybrids of grass, everything sharp, loud, bright, big, smart, and very expensive.

We take more care of a ball field than we do of the church.

If someone should argue that the ball field requires only prefabricated sections of this and that to be pieced together, while the church requires real craftsmanship from the human hand, I must reply that this is no answer at all. Is it not true that hundreds of thousands of men who could support families by the skill in their hands do not do so now because we do not ask for those skills, except in the rare cases of homes for the wealthiest among us? We are servile for mass entertainment, when we could be free with our hearts and ourselves for the worship of God, which truly builds up a human community, rather than just herding people in an aggregate of many thousands who do not know one another, and whose only common bond is that they prefer a certain style of uniform.

But why would we care to make our churches beautiful when what goes on in them is slipshod and is not felt to be of even temporal consequence, let alone eternal? We do nothing in the week that is more significant than to serve God by prayer. That is a fact. We have forgotten it. Our hearts skip a beat when someone gives us a surprise ticket to the baseball game. Those same hearts plod along at their usual sluggish tempo when we dress for church, if we dress for church at all. So we end up with stadiums that will not last twenty years before the owners of the ball club demand new ones. Chartres Cathedral has been standing for eight hundred years.

Think of it, everyone—preachers, parishioners, choristers, artists.

THREE

A MIND IS A TERRIBLE THING TO BASTE:
Restoring the School

One summer my family and I visited Orwell Corners, the site of an old farming village on Prince Edward Island. If there is anything that English-speakers know about the island, it is that Lucy Maud Montgomery lived there and used it as the setting for her stories about Anne Shirley, the orphan girl and eponymous heroine of *Anne of Green Gables* and a spate of other novels. Anne is an excellent student, and in fact much of the interest of the novels centers around the life of the mind—whether Anne's friendship with her fellow student Diana, her rivalry and then her deepening regard for Gilbert Blythe, or her having to balance her longing to learn with her duties to the family that opened its home to her. Perhaps that explains the enormous popularity of the books in Japan, that land of studiousness, especially among Japanese women, several of whom we saw in the lobby of our hotel.

The rich red clay of Prince Edward Island was good for growing potatoes and serious Presbyterians. That became clear to us at Orwell

Corners. There was a one-room schoolhouse on the site, something that is irresistible to me and my family. It opened in 1895 and closed only late, in 1969. The village too "closed," that is, the people moved away, so that what is there now is a restoration. But the woman who worked the general store told us that she was among the last graduates of the school, in the year when it closed. She loved that school dearly. I have met a few people who attended one-room schools, and every one of them has beamed with gratitude and delight, remembering the peculiar features: boys chopping wood for the burner; a two-seater outhouse in the back; the older students sometimes helping the younger with their lessons; the younger overhearing the lessons of their elders and learning them almost before they learned them; everyone knowing everyone and their families; play in the yard before and after; a feeling of being home.

In their justified pride, the caretakers of the schoolhouse, now a museum piece of Canadiana, had collected actual lessons written up by the first students of the school in 1895. I don't think they offered these artifacts as a reproach to the modern world, but they surely were that. Two of the lessons stand out in my mind. Each took up a single sheet of paper. One of them was headed by a couple of verses of devotional poetry. Beneath the verses, the student had parsed every word in the verses, describing what part of speech it was, what grammatical form it bore (case, number, and gender for nouns and adjectives; person, number, tense, mood, and voice for verbs), what function it served in its clause, and what relation it bore to other words. The student's performance was entirely correct. The other lesson was obviously an introductory one: the student wrote a noun in its singular and plural forms, in the nominative, genitive, dative, and accusative cases. This second student was clearly one of the younger children, as you could tell from an occasional roughness in his printing. The word in question was *doulos*: Greek for "servant." The children were evidently studying *koine* Greek, so as to be able to read the New Testament in the original tongue.

I will give more examples of what our schools *once taught*. But that is not my first point here. Sure, none of my college freshmen, except for those very few who have both studied Latin and been instructed in

Latin's relations to English, knows any grammar. There is no grammar in grammar school, and there is not much school there, either. Yet before we even get to that, we have to address the massive *thing* that stares out at us from its fifty blank windows. It is not that Prince Edward Island has changed, in the way that an organism grows and develops its latent capacities. It is not that *the school* has changed, as a young lad will find his voice dropping into the tenor and the baritone, while his arms and legs and shoulders catch up with his hands and feet, and youth blooms and flourishes and becomes manhood in its prime. It is that that old Prince Edward Island is dead, and the old place called *school* is dead. A monstrous thing has taken its place—not just a parasite or a cancer feeding off the host, but a disease that has slowly transformed the host into itself, like an all-eating and all-digesting alien. The word *school* remains, but not the reality.

Try to imagine someone armed with directives from Ottawa marching up to Anne Shirley, now a teacher, and telling her that she must instruct the little boys in "sexual expression" and "transgender rights." When she narrows her eyes and wonders who gave the government official the authority to dictate to her what is best for her charges, rendering their parents irrelevant and obnoxiously presuming to overrule nature itself, she is subject to a barrage of contempt—from someone who has not one fiftieth of her knowledge of arts and letters or of the human realities of men and women, boys and girls. If Anne of Green Gables persists, she is fired and replaced by someone—usually a woman, call her Susie of the Sex Shop—who is strangely *eager* to impart this instruction, though we may question her equal eagerness to impart what little knowledge she may have of poetry or Scripture or British history.

Try to imagine explaining to the old farmers of Prince Edward Island the need to teach small children how to insert, safely of course, antiseptically of course, their fingers or tongues or other protuberances into the orifice of another kid of ambiguous sex, including the anus. It is not that they would *disagree* with you. It is not that they would have an *alternative opinion* about behavior that makes old-fashioned sodomy look like a peck on the cheek. It is that they would think that you had lost your mind. They would believe that you were suffering a terrifying moral and psychological illness, nigh unto demonic possession, or perhaps well past it. Would they let you speak to their children? They would not want you to speak to their *parents* or friends or anybody, not because they would be afraid that you might persuade or entice one of them, but merely to spare their loved ones the experience of something so gross, so wicked, so repulsive, so sad. They themselves, in future years, would let the memory of it drop into the darkness and the silence. You do not make scrapbooks of slime.

Now the question for us is not *whether* perversion ought to be taught in school. Nor is it even whether teachers should instruct small children in how to behave like a member of the opposite sex. Let us change the terms of the situation so that we can see what the problem really is. Suppose it is not sex we are talking about, but violence. Imagine a world in which teachers introduce children to the thrill-seeking of stabbing and slashing—with precautions, of course, so that the person who is stabbed will probably not bleed to death. Suppose the teachers bring to the school speakers who delight in cruelty, whose eyes shine when they recount the first time they gouged out the eye of an enemy. Imagine that parents are not even informed when a machete-wielding gang man demonstrates on stage the proper angle at which to slice off someone's arm in mid-fight. Imagine safe switchblades.

The problem is that you would be dealing with people whose imaginations and moral sensibilities are so diseased as to make such things even conceivable. It will not do merely to restrain them in this or that regard. They are not fit to teach your children the multiplication table. They are not fit to be near them at all. Every moment that your children are in their presence, they will be breathing the putrescent air from the diseased heart and spirit of the instructors, in an institution whose walls stink of it, it has lingered there so long. We are not talking about sinners here, since everyone is one of those. We are talking about people whom C. S. Lewis called the "bent," those whose souls are warped, so that the more "honest" and consistent and idealistic they are, the worse they will be; just as a faithful adherent of Stalin is far worse than an inconsistent adherent of Churchill, and more dangerous than someone who is too selfish or too stupid to be an adherent of anyone at all.

But the problem is even worse than that. No such person could ever be hired in the first place unless the entire school system were not slavering for him—or, more frequently these days, her. From top to bottom the system is laced with people whose imaginations have been corrupted. If that were not bad enough already, the publishers of textbooks and exams know it and provide them with their materials accordingly. The evil is not just here or there, in this teacher or that, on this day or that, when this subject or that comes up, in this school or that school. It is everywhere, a pervasive pollution, like fecal bacteria in your water supply.

Is that bad enough? Return to the small schoolhouse in Nova Scotia.

We can tell quite a lot from the assignments of those two children. There is a natural order at work, and a moral and intellectual order. Outside of the schoolhouse in the early morning the robins, thrushes they, though the thrush-speckles of their chests have grown into the brick orange of their maturity, sing in the lower branches of the trees. The warm smell of ripening grain is in the air. The boys sit on one side, the girls on the other. One of the boys makes a teasing face at a girl across the way. She makes one back at him. Evidently they are meant to be married someday. Then the teacher leads them in a short prayer, and the day begins. She asks the older children here, ten or eleven years, to begin with their next Greek lesson, on page fourteen. She asks the younger children there, six or seven years, to take out their readers and begin on the second lesson, a little poem about summertime. In a few minutes, three or four separate lessons are going on, most of them silently. She walks about, speaking in a low and gentle voice so as not to disturb the children at their work, helping, giving hints, encouraging, prompting.

We are witnessing here not a *different way* of doing something that is still done now. We might as well be walking into another world entirely. Everything taught here and everything done here is oriented towards the worship of God, the beauty of the noblest human arts, the life of the mind, and the pursuit of the common good. We may well imagine the same young people, reaching the age of Anne Shirley, plowing the fields, singing at church, reading together the latest novel by Thomas Hardy, discussing the merits of democracy or constitutional monarchy, putting on a masquerade party with everyone dressed up as somebody from history, passing around sheet music for songs by Debussy, the men playing hockey on a frozen pond or sawing out blocks for the ice house, the women talking for hours and hours as they stitch quilts together.

The schoolhouse at Orwell Corners on that small foggy island was a place of real culture. Spell out the declension of a Greek noun? Our teachers cannot parse an English noun. Say a prayer? Our teachers wave rainbow banners for Sodom and Gomorrah; they not only do not pray, they would not know how to begin. Read the poetry of Tennyson or Browning? Discuss the cultural theories of Matthew Arnold? Study Plutarch's *Lives*? How can children learn to do what their teachers cannot do or refuse to do?

What do our schools do well? Teach history? Forget it—literally, forget it. History is scorned as a long string of evils perpetrated against the favored groups of the day. Teach geography? That subject has been abandoned. The boys and girls on Prince Edward Island, who could not travel more than a hundred miles without getting on a boat, knew more about the world than our students do. Lead students into the wonders of English literature? Most of that before 1900 was poetry, and poetry also has been abandoned. Why should we be surprised by this? If you don't even believe in the objective existence of beauty, you aren't going to incline to teach students to love it.

—There are only two things wrong with our schools: everything that our children don't learn there and everything they do. The public schools, with their vast political and bureaucratic machinery, are beyond reform. That does not mean that persons of good will should not offer themselves up as missionaries of truth and goodness and beauty, to teach there, as *in partibus furibundis*. But we would be quite mad to send our children there. We send missionaries to cannibals. We do not serve the cannibals our boys and girls.

The Form of Learning: The Shape of the School

We must then build new schools. We have no alternative. How then shall we build them?

I return to the schoolhouse at Orwell Corners. The twentieth-century masters of some of the world's most brutal architecture said they wanted to create "machines" for this and that, including Le Corbusier's "machines for living." Well, we do not want machines for teaching, for the obvious reason that we are not teaching machines, nor are they machines whom we teach. They are, at first, little boys and girls.

The schoolhouse at Orwell Corners looked much like its sister schools all over North America. It was painted white, with one big room inside. It had high clear windows, so that natural light would stream in. It was gabled, like a house. It had a bell, like a church. It bore signs of patriotic love, like a town hall. It was like those things— the home, the church, and the town meeting place— because the children were the small members of homes and a church and a town. It was intimate, like a home, and civic, like the town hall, and oriented towards the highest and noblest things, like a church. Its very shape reflected the nature of the small people to be taught there, and of the big people who sent them, and of the reality—natural and social and sacred—round about them. We would not say, with Frank Lloyd Wright, that the form of the school followed upon its *function*. We would say that *form followed essence*.

So let us concentrate first on form—not this or that form, but the fact of form itself. The schoolhouse has a recognizable form. It is not a sprawling factory, covering half an acre, amorphous, like a thing out of a nightmare. It is beautiful, and we are not surprised to find that beauty dwells within it also.

We enter, and we find the young pupils engaged in the unfolding of beauty. They are not yet aware of it, because they have not yet mastered the code. I am not talking here about phonetics, which is a matter of course. English is not Chinese. English is not written in pictograms. It has an alphabet, which the boys and girls have mastered. But the alphabet is only the beginning. Learning the alphabet is like removing a blanket from around a treasure chest. It does not open the chest.

"But it allows the children to read," you say, and I agree that it does—to a point. It allows them to fumble about the sides of the treasure chest, and to investigate some outer pockets here and there. That is a good and proper thing. They should certainly learn how to decipher the letters on a page, so that they can read English words, and even those strings of English words we call sentences. But there is more, much more.

It is strange but true that most of our teachers at this point will not know what I am talking about. Once you have learned to read, all that remains, they believe, is to be exposed—like a silver plate left out in a smoky room?—to be exposed, I say, to more and more "complex" writing, the complexity gauged by various algorithms that count the number of words per sentence and the number of syllables per word. We know that the children will have achieved full "proficiency"—notice the industrial noun—if they can make sense out of the sludge of somebody's sociological essay on the rates of incarceration for city dwellers in pre-Columbian Mexico. Far from opening the chest, *that* lugs it into a closet, locks the door, loses the key, and then forgets that there ever was a treasure to begin with.

Return to the schoolhouse. Is it not also strange but true that you would never expect to find a box filled with beautiful and precious things in a plastics plant or a modern school, but you might find one in somebody's home, or in a church, or even in a small old town hall, fallen into disuse? What are the boys and girls doing in the school at Orwell Corners? They are not being trained in the ugly and the stupid, as the unrelated Orwell named George would say fifty years later. They are learning grammar.

To the untutored, and therefore to most of our teachers, there is no beauty to grammar. What they know of grammar, which is little enough, is an unorganized heap of apparently arbitrary rules, many of them incorrect at that. Grammar, for them, resembles not the schoolhouse, nor a treasure chest, but the sprawling factory, or perhaps the dirt and rocks plowed up in order to build the factory, which now serve as landfill for what used to be a wonderfully gloomy ravine behind the building. Grammar for them is not *architectonic*: it does not build, it does not relate one thing to another, it does not shed light everywhere. But they are wrong. The beginning of grammar is the key that opens the treasure chest, and inside that chest the first things we see—and they are gleaming in plain sight—are *other keys,* the grammatical and architectonic keys not only to English but to human language itself. We teach grammar because we want our children to be the masters of language.

Let me give an example or two. My college students have been taught, most of them, never to use the passive voice. That's dreadful advice, because people invented the passive voice for good reasons; look at my previous sentence, after all. I wanted the focus of the sentence to be the subject, because I'm talking about what my students know and don't know. It would add nothing to the sentence if I had placed the agent of the verb, "their teachers," in the position as subject, because that is understood from the context already. It would get in the way. So there are excellent reasons for using the passive voice. But very few of my students can even define what that thing is which they are not supposed to use! They "know" that it has something or other to do with the verb *be,* but that is an accidental feature of English and has nothing to do, per se, with the passive. In Latin and Greek and Hebrew, the passive is marked by a change on the verb, and *be* has nothing to do with it. Meanwhile, because my students do not really understand the linguistic concept of voice, they end up thinking that all uses of the verb *be* are to be proscribed. That produces the dreadful habit of finding synonyms for that most convenient little verb: most notoriously and incorrectly, *exists.*

So their prose is worse than nature ever intended even a dullard's to be, *and they still have learned nothing about language.* "Voice," says the teacher who knows what she is talking about, "describes what is going on between the subject and the verb. Johnny, stand here."

Johnny obliges, smiling.

"Now Billy, take that baseball I know you have it stashed in your bag—I know it's there, no pretending! Toss it to Johnny."

He does, and Johnny catches the ball.

"Billy threw the baseball. What's the verb in that sentence? Billy threw the baseball. Amy?"

"The verb is *threw*."

"That is correct. How did you know that?"

"Because," says Amy, "the verb names the action."

"Very good. Now, who was active in the throwing? Who was doing the verb? Was it the ball? Was the ball throwing?"

"No!" the class laughs in chorus.

"No, of course not. *Billy* threw the baseball. The subject threw the baseball. The subject was doing the throwing. The subject was acting. That is what we call the *active voice,* when the subject is the doer of the verb, when the subject puts the verb into action or into being. Billy is a boy. The verb is active, because Billy the subject is being a boy. The action goes *this way*," and she grabs Billy by the shoulders and hustles him across the room, laughing.

"Repeat after me, everyone: the subject acts, active voice." The children do so. "We will learn about the *passive voice* tomorrow. Can anyone guess what it might be?"

And so forth. In that schoolhouse in Orwell Corners, it is impossible that the schoolteacher could be confused about the elements of English grammar. You do not take two steps in ancient Greek without it.

Let no one object that the lesson I have described is pointless, just an exercise in pedantic definition. Is it pedantic definition to know what mortar is, and how to lay it smooth on a row of bricks? Grammar is more than the brick and mortar of language. It is what imparts force to our words: the slender nerves that send their signals to every cell in the body, without which there would be no organism at all, but only a heap, an aggregate of muscle and bone and guts and blood.

But I have said that grammar is a set of keys—that it opens. It *is not* true that every human language has all the same grammatical organs, though there are many (nouns, verbs) without which language is inconceivable. It *is* true that to learn to think grammatically in your mother tongue gives you the opportunity to think grammatically in another tongue. The children may be fascinated to learn that verbs have voice, which in English we designate as active and passive. What may be their wonder when they learn that Greek has a middle voice, wherein the action proceeds from the subject but remains also within the subject? When they hear such a thing, they might stop; not stop *something else,* which would be active, nor *be stopped* as by a policeman at a street corner, which would be passive, but just—*stop,* like that, right in the middle.

My students often say that they learned what little they know of English grammar very late in their years; at about the age when boys used to go to Harvard, a couple of years older than John Quincy Adams was when he returned to America from Russia, having transacted diplomatic business there in French, as a teenager whose voice had probably not yet changed. I am grateful for the occasional dismembered grammatical finger or toe that my students have thus scrambled up. Yet even that is not too common. If they have studied a modern language, the "conversational" method rules, which means that after four years of Spanish they might be able to ask for the bathrooms in Tijuana, but they will not be able to read Cervantes, nor will they be able to compose more than the most childish letter. The keepers in our asylums have little use for Cervantes. They do not tilt at windmills. Unless we are talking about sex, they do not tilt at much of anything.

So a study of English grammar hands them a set of keys called *other languages,* and each one of those opens a couple of doors in turn. One of those doors is to a room filled with what looks like the most outlandish objects, but a second glance tells you that they are odd lamps, goblets, tea trays, chairs, toys, bookends, andirons, a sideboard, a hat rack, a bear rug with the bear still half in it, and so on. They are curiosities, because your curiosity is what they stir, and delightfully so. "She brought her first born son *to the light,*" they say in Portuguese; what a fine way of expressing the birth of the Christ child, or of any child! "Come *there-out,* right now," calls the German mother to her mischievous daughter who has turned the big cupboard into a secret room of her own. "I see you've got mice in your corn crib," says Davy the Welsh farmer to his neighbor. "A good *earth-dog* might take care of that," he says, while his own earth-dog, a Scottie, snuffles about the place with wary excitement. That is not to be confused with the Afrikaans *earth-hog,* the great anteater.

"Hail, Caesar!" cry the gladiators before the daily competition and butchery. "Morituri te salutamus!" We who are about to die salute thee! And there Latin expressed in a single word, the future active participle *morituri*, a notion that takes up four or five words in English. Quite a useful thing to have around. Billy, now a couple of years older, furrows his brow. "Miss Shirley," he says, "if there's a future active participle, can there be a future passive participle too?" She nods and smiles. "Not only can there be," she says, "but there certainly is, and it gives us plenty of words in English, some of which I'll bet you know already." And in the minds of the boy and his fellow students the language-world beneath them seems to come into sharper view, its rivers and dells and plains and hills all in recognizable order, as if they were surveying it from a mountain in the morning while the mists were clearing away.

But we have only begun to investigate the grammatical keys. I have said that grammar is an architectonic thing, and I mean it in all seriousness. Consider other areas of learning that are like grammar or that have a deep grammar that informs them, that rules what you can do and what you cannot, that gives you the beams and joists of the building of knowledge. Geography—also abandoned by the schools as a subject in its own right—is like that. There are continents, not arbitrarily designated but actual land masses each with its own peculiar characteristics, and in the continents there are nations, more or less congruent with people who speak the same languages and share the same history and culture; and in the nations there are provinces or states or cantons, and in those there are counties, and cities, and towns, and villages. On the rivers there are ports, and if the river is deep and without rapids or falls, those ports can be as far as two thousand miles from the sea (Minneapolis). In the deserts there are oases, and if you have such a place that is convenient for caravans crossing from a couple of directions, you may end up with an important trading post (Timbuktu). On the seacoast there are harbors, depending upon the action of the water and the general direction of the winds and the underlying features of the land, whether flat or mountainous; and if the seawater makes its way far into the coast, you have a perfect site for ships (Narragansett Bay). In the sea there are islands, mountains that poke their heads above the water (Hawaii), or large areas of what was once mainland but is now cut off by the sinking of the land bridge that connected it long ago (Madagascar).

To be adept at grammar, to learn how to think in structures of meaning, to be able to map out a sentence, is to be on your way to making maps properly speaking, and to be on your way to mapping out many other things too. *All human sciences are grammatical in structure.* Basic chemistry is a grammar whose elements are the elements, arranged in several orders at once in the periodic table, and a lad who knows what a periodic sentence is will know why the table has that name. There are rules, not arbitrary conventions, that bind one element to another in a compound. There is a deep structure to each element's basic molecule, and this structure helps determine the element's action in concert with other elements. I am writing these words on a computer that could have been invented only by men who looked hard at the crystal and electro-chemical properties of that semi-conducting semi-metallic element, silicon. *Only* an element with the "grammatical" structure of silicon would do the trick.

Biology is a grammar too. It is not an accident that the first biologists, like Cuvier and Linnaeus, were *taxonomists*, people who organized the exuberant lushness of nature into observable and rational categories, from the "continental" kingdoms to the towns and neighborhoods we call genera and species. They did not do this to be pedantic. They did it to understand: to see that the purple finch is in the same clan as the cardinal, but that you have to broaden your sights a bit, or rise up to the next grammatical level, to see that the finch is more closely related to the sparrow than to the eagle, more closely related to the eagle than to the snake, more closely related to the snake than to the bear, more closely related to the bear than to the jellyfish, and so on. Nor have scientists abandoned this ordering. Find a new species of fish, and you will be hailed across the scientific world. Argue that what was formerly considered to be a separate species is not separate at all, and you will make scientific headlines, and sometimes draw scientific blood. I can imagine devoted grammarians heaving books at each other's heads.

Even such a pastime as chess is grammatical: it is systematic, with rules, and what the lovers of the game call "lines" (trains of moves in certain situations), "openings" (such as the Ruy Lopez and the King's Gambit Declined), defenses, sacrifices, and so on. The masters understand that sophisticated games of chess fall into a broad variety of categories and sub-categories, reaching down to a slight change in the seventh move by one of the players, and they have *names* for the variations, so that their experience of the game passes into study, knowledge, and creativity.

At this point we might well wonder whether as great a thing as *existence* is not grammatical. Our ancestors thought so. That was the insight behind their great scale or ladder of being. God is the sole necessary being; all other beings are created and contingent. Among those creatures, some are intellectual and incorporeal, others are intellectual (or rational—at least we hope so) and corporeal, others are subrational. Among the subrational, some have perception and memory (dogs) and some do not (grass). And we go on, down to the grain of sand, or the electron, or the quark, or whatever other infinitesimal spark or tickle there may be near absolute grammatical zero.

The Town Hall

I have said that the schoolhouse at Orwell Corners looked something like a town hall. I believe there were a few noticeable tokens of the nation there: a portrait of the first prime minister of the Dominion, John A. MacDonald, and hymn books boasting that melodious anthem, "O Canada."

Here we must draw distinctions. The schools we have built in the last sixty or seventy years do not resemble town halls. If they resemble anything governmental, it is the *bureau,* the *office building,* where human business goes to be swallowed up, as Charlie Chaplin's little factory worker in *Modern Times* is swallowed up in the gigantic gears of the mill or as the girl dancer in *Return of the Jedi,* after pleasing His Immensity, is swallowed up by Jabba the Hutt. We never sense, when we are in a governmental office building, that we are the creators and the masters of the government. We sense that we are its wards, its clients, and perhaps its victims and its food. The emotion we feel most powerfully is not confidence or a sense of our authority, but fear. The proper relationship is reversed. We see this reversal quite clearly whenever a parent, who ought to be considered the teacher's employer, or the one who delegates his authority to the teacher under certain conditions that he and his fellow parents stipulate, attempts to register a complaint about some nonsense or perversion or even attempts to set foot on the school grounds without permission. The educrats in Ottawa are quite open about what they believe the children to be: *theirs,* and the parents' only under sufferance.

In other words, the schools we have built are monstrosities that reflect the government we have built, a government that has taken on an all-eating life of its own.

The old town hall is not a monstrosity. That place was near to the people who built it with their own hands, stone upon stone. That was where the people who created the town would meet to discuss their common affairs. What shall we do about the stream that has overflowed its banks and is now soaking some excellent fields? The fire truck is old and always in danger of breaking down when we need it. What kind of replacement shall we buy? How shall we raise the money for it? The pastor says that there is a family in a village nearby in great need—the man of the house has died of pneumonia, the woman is ill, and there are six children, all of them under twelve years old, three boys and three girls. Can anyone take some of them in?

The old town hall was not made by a Town Hall Bureaucracy, a National Town Hall Association, which of course is a contradiction in terms. It was made by the people of the town, for their purposes. A school that resembles that town hall also reflects the purposes of its builders. It is not Ottawa's school. It is *their school.* They are its proprietors and overseers. They hire the teacher. They examine and approve the books. They put their sweat into it, and their hearts and minds.

So the school then ushers the young people into a truly social and cultural world. It is not the world of mass education, mass politics, and mass entertainment, but the world of Orwell Corners, then Prince Edward Island, then Canada, and the British Empire. They are citizens of a country, and the first order of the history-teaching business is to introduce them to their country's noble past. It is not necessary that children should be taught that their nation is the greatest that the world has ever seen. By what measure could we even make that claim? Unless he is taught otherwise, by some serpent of envy or by a cynical dog snuffling about in the alleys for garbage, the child will naturally love his country, just as he naturally loves his mother and father, not because they are perfect, but because they are *his*.

I am not talking about sprinkling sugar upon that history—or slathering it with acid. All nations bear the mark of mankind. We are fools and sinners, and there will be plenty of time for children to learn that hard lesson, just as they will learn that there are times when mother is difficult and father inattentive, and that parents too can get things wrong. But it is the essence of piety to honor your father and mother *because they are yours* and because they have given you a gift you can never recompense. This piety extends to the land of your birth, the "rocks and rills," the "templed hills," as the old patriotic anthem has it. The character of a nation is not to be found primarily in great political movements, and certainly not in an obsession with "progress." It is found in its land and weather, the kind of people who work there, the music they sing, the places where they worship, the games they play, the food they raise; what they honor and love, and what they will shed their blood to save.

The town hall suggests as much. It says to the citizen, "This is your home too." Every child is born into a web of relationships extending far into the past. Other animals float along on the current of time. Man alone dwells in time and makes it his: he builds up a history.

The word *story* comes from the Latin *historia*, and that is just as well. History for children is a grand story filled with stories, and the names and the dates are important in the story for the same reason that you cannot make any sense out of a novel if you are always forgetting who is who and how old they are. For the last hundred years, educational innovators have been telling us that history is more than a matter of names and dates, as if anybody ever said it was. The result is that students don't know any of those names and dates, *and* because they have no cast of characters and no timeline, they can't tell any stories, either. (Bones alone do not a body make, but if you have no bones at all, you might be able to float in the water like a jellyfish, shlup shlup, but that is about it.) If you look at an old town hall, it will occur to you at once that the place might house *stories*. Who is that august personage in the fading portrait? What is that document under the glass case? What names are on that memorial? When was that picture taken, the one where the men seem to be cutting a ribbon near a railroad track?

When we are children, we want to hear about what things were like when our parents and grandparents were young. Is that not in itself remarkable? We fail to appreciate it only because it is as common as the blue sky above us. We are too accustomed to wonders. Why should a child care about the time when his grandfather, a young man, boasted to a recent Italian immigrant that he could order somebody's death and it would happen with a snap of the fingers? It wasn't true; it was all bluster meant to impress and fool the newcomer, but that is what my father's father did. It did not make my grandfather a great man, and it certainly did not make him a good man, but it made him human, and helped me form a clearer picture of him in my mind. I see him in the studio photograph mounted behind glass and hung on the wall of their parlor. He is short, dark, lean, and glowering. He is wearing the uniform he wore when he served in the army in World War I—the American army. And I wonder what it was like for him, speaking broken English, to serve alongside Americans in a war waged on the other side of the ocean, and partly in Italy at that.

Now we can see how inhuman it is to project history onto the flat template of political action or political ideology. We do not, in the first instance, want to know about the politics behind Ellis Island; we want to know the stories of the people. But to know people in a story requires of us an act of the moral imagination. We want to know what it was like to be a good man on the wrong side: the godly and beloved and dauntless Stonewall Jackson; the man of impeccable honor, Robert E. Lee. We want to know what it was like to be a man with grave moral failings, like Andrew Jackson, but with considerable virtues and personal magnetism and an iron will. We want to honor heroism wherever we find it. It is easy enough to find vices and weakness. We need only look in the mirror.

When he was shot by a crazed anarchist, William McKinley, that man with the hard features and the beetling brows, whom his political opponents accused of being an agent of boundless corporate rapacity, begged the people round him not to hurt his assassin and then asked his secretary to break the news gently to his invalid wife, Ida, whom he loved very dearly. Teddy Roosevelt had once accused McKinley of being "yellow" because the president was slow to declare war against Spain when all America, and especially Teddy, was spoiling for a fight. That same Roosevelt, now vice president in McKinley's second term, heard the news of the shooting while he was vacationing in upstate New York. The president died after several days; had modern medicine been available, he might well have lived. Roosevelt became president, and he had no nagging moral qualms about America's assuming a position of dominance on the international stage. It is a human story, one that our students should know.

Our young people should march with Hannibal over the Alps. Who would have thought of hacking a pass through the mountains with elephants along for the journey? How could they keep any of the beasts from hurtling to their deaths along the icy ridges? Our young people should be huddling with Robert Falcon Scott as his frostbitten fingers scribble out the last entry in his diary before he dies in the Antarctic. What possessed him to try to reach the South Pole? Why did he take ponies along rather than mush-dogs only, as did his rival Roald Amundsen? They should stand with Balboa as he mounts the hill in Panama and sees the great Pacific Ocean for the first time. History is not our current political neuralgia in the past tense. That would make it into a long and tedious allegory of the worst sort, one whose characters in their humanity disappear as soon as you apply to them your allegorical decoder ring: hence George Washington, one of the greatest men that any nation has ever brought forth, will be reduced to a somewhat intelligent fellow who happened to be at the beginning of a great experiment in social liberation or what have you. When you are keeping watch at the bedside of a dying man, it would be not only impertinent, it would border upon the sociopathic, were to you keep asking whether he voted Democrat or Republican and what he believed about the rights of women and minorities.

Politics can come later. Aristotle said that young men—much older than our children in school—were not yet ready to study politics, because they had not yet amassed any great experience of human nature. That is what literature is for, and history also; a story of stories.

The School Bell

The public high school that my mother attended in the town where I was born no longer stands. A small park with a memorial is in its place. The school was a few hundred feet away from the Catholic church, the rectory, the parish school, and the convent of the nuns who taught there. The people of my town had a strong sense that these enterprises were bound up together, so that once a week the teachers at the public school, when the day's classes were over, would see to it that the Catholic students marched across the street to the parochial school for religious instruction. Nobody thought that that was untoward. Nobody feared some sinister cooperation of the religious with the secular. It was a matter of course.

It was also a matter of course that the high school had a belfry. I have said that the old schoolhouse in Orwell Corners resembled a town hall. It also resembled a spare and handsome Presbyterian church. The high school in Archbald, Pennsylvania, resembled a Catholic chapel. In the belfry, or you might call it a steeple, was a big bell, for ringing the hour when school started or when it resumed after recess. It was a bell and not an alarm. It tolled in the same way that a church bell would toll. An alarm summons nameless masses to their task. A church bell summons human beings to the worship of God. An alarm is a veiled threat. A church bell is a solemn welcome.

In fact it is a sign that you are among civilized people and not savages or brutes. In Shakespeare's *As You Like It,* the hero Orlando, wandering in the Forest of Arden with his loyal old servant Adam and desperate to find him something to eat, comes upon a band of men about to sit down to supper. He assumes that they are outlaws and at first threatens them with his sword, but when they speak to him kindly, he begs them for food if they are true human beings and not beasts, if they have ever seen better days than these, doing the sorts of things that decent people would do. The leader of the band, the gracious and noble Duke Senior, replies:

> True it is we have seen better days,
> And have with holy bell been knolled to church,
> And sat at good men's feasts, and wiped our eyes
> Of drops that sacred pity hath engendered.

The health of a society may be gauged by how full the churches are, those beating hearts of culture and communion.

A school built in the form of a chapel and inspired by something like religious devotion will be open to the transcendent. It is not just that an antiseptic place will be scrubbed out for a little bit of talk about religion now and again when the odd subject comes up in history or literature. For the role of religion in human life is not *little*. It is essential: without it there is no culture at all, because culture is a cultivation of the things that a people considers most sacred. Those who talk glibly about the "multicultural" are, in my experience, mainly monolingual Westerners who have lost any strong sense of what any kind of culture must be about. Their "culture" is culinary or epidermal. They are tourists at best, self-satisfied and patronizing, sampling a little jazz on Tuesday and a little Japanese watercolor on Wednesday, and always remaining stolidly certain that the whole world is moving toward their own supposedly progressive ideals—and if it is not, there are always armies, dollars, and food to make damned sure it does. Thus does the "multicultural" act as a universal cultural solvent. So too the "progressive" drive to bleach religious devotion out of whatever remains of the culture to be handed on to children in school. The result is not white and pure, but blank and void.

Imagine having children exercise every day so that their bodies will be strong and fit—but indoors, always indoors. Or imagine studying the art of painting—in black and white. Or imagine studying classical music, but with the piano and the violins taken out. Imagine being sent to Nepal, but staying in the airport and never standing upon a mountaintop. Imagine going deep-sea fishing, with a rod, a string, and some worms.

To take the highest things out of a curriculum is to attempt to win a temporary consensus by sacrificing what the education of a human being ultimately is for. We avoid religious questions at the cost of avoiding the most human questions. And thus education, which should be human, is reduced to the mechanical and the low.

An example will suffice. You are teaching English literature. Can you teach Chaucer? If you do, you will have to explain what a pilgrimage is, why the pilgrims are going to the shrine of Saint Thomas Becket at Canterbury, why the Lenten "drought of March" has given way to April and Eastertide, why the Parson ends the tales with a disquisition on penance, delivered on the evening of the third day as they round the bend and come within sight of Canterbury Cathedral. You will have to explain why the Pardoner's sales line, *radix malorum est cupiditas*—the root of evil is cupidity—does not exactly mean what he intends it to mean. You will have to talk about the meaning of the Eucharist. You will have to tell the students why John the carpenter in the Miller's Tale is especially foolish for believing that Noah's or "Noel's" flood is returning to wipe out all of mankind. You will have to show them the anti-Eden in the Merchant's Tale. You will have to explain why Chaucer chose Bath as the place where his irrepressible Wife came from, and what that has to do with a multitude of husbands.

Just to make sense of that great and unique poetic masterpiece, you will have to talk about the Christian faith; but if you want the students to love the poem, the faith cannot remain a mere source of information. In some sense the students will have to enter imaginatively into Chaucer's point of view. They will have to go on that pilgrimage in spirit. You cannot read Shakespeare's *The Tempest* unless you understand the Christian narrative of sin, punishment, repentance, forgiveness, and resurrection, and you cannot really love it unless that narrative moves you to the core of your being. There is little left of English literature if the religious is barred at the door. Dickens wrote with the Gospels always near his heart: "Suffer the little children to come unto me, and forbid them not; for of such is the kingdom of God." Robert Browning was a restlessly religious poet, always searching; hence his "Epistle of Karshish," ostensibly written by a Syrian physician to one of his colleagues, about a doctor he has heard tell of who the people say raised a man from the dead, or his "Cleon," a letter from a minor Greek philosopher, shedding light upon the dead-ends of first-century philosophy, yet looking down upon a Jewish teacher named Paul who has been making a stir in the Hellenic world.

You won't be teaching Eliot's "The Hollow Men," inspired by the nameless empty souls in the vestibule of Dante's *Inferno*, or "Ash Wednesday," "The Return of the Magi," and *Murder in the Cathedral*. Forget about "The Waste Land." Forget about Tennyson's "In Memoriam" and the poet's mighty struggle to see the hand of God in the world, amidst his profound personal loss. Forget about Spenser, Milton, Donne, Herbert, Johnson, and Bunyan. If you cross the English Channel or the North Sea, you can forget about Cervantes, Manzoni, Dostoyevsky, Tolstoy, and Goethe. The great questions of human existence are and always will be religious, whatever the answers might be that one culture or another, or one author or another, may have ventured. Josef Pieper says that in the whole history of man there is no celebration, properly speaking, without the gods, no matter how tenuous the association may have become. We may say also that in the whole history of man there is no education of a human soul unless the divine animates it. Otherwise it is mere training, fit for a dog, or habituation, fit for a machine, or political indoctrination, fit for no creature that has ever breathed upon earth.

Let us look to it, then. We need not invent a new thing in the world. We are not imagining a castle in the air. We need only restore a very old and venerable thing in the world, with its foundation solidly laid in the God-created earth, and its spire pointing towards the place where man is meant to turn.

FOUR

MAN BY NATURE DESIRES TO KNOW:
Rebuilding the College

Our schools are mostly a dead loss. Our colleges are not much healthier. Any dispassionate observer must conclude that higher education in the United States, and in many other Western nations, is in a bad way. I am not talking about troubles that are easily remedied or errors that require adjustment and reform. I am talking about whether higher education as the West has known it for eight hundred years is any longer possible.

The frieze beneath the rotunda of the state house at Providence, the city where my college is located, proclaims, in the words of Tacitus, the happiness of the times when a man "may think what he will and speak what he thinks." This may still be true of men sitting at a diner or a bar, drinking beer and arguing about politics. Rational argument and freedom of thought, like the exercise of religion, has retreated into the realm of the private. You may still think what you will, so long as you keep it to yourself. You may not think or speak freely in our political assemblies, our newspapers, and our colleges.

Here the reader may supply plenty of anecdotes about professors, insufficiently "liberal," who have been driven from their jobs or burdened with legal troubles because they violated the new iron etiquette that governs the public sphere. My favorite, if such it may be called, involved an instructor of composition at the University of Winnipeg who remarked, near the end of a semester, that the most important work that most women do will be to raise their children well. For that remark—which would have struck sensible people alive three cultural minutes ago, both men and women, as a bland truism—the instructor was relieved of his duties forthwith, barred from his office, and forbidden even to administer his final exam.

People who say that such events are rare and therefore not to be taken too seriously are either fools or liars. A thousand public lynchings are expensive and tiresome. Two or three will intimidate your enemies very nicely and save you the sweat and the struggle against your conscience. That is especially true if the victim is powerful and visible, as was Lawrence Summers, the president of Harvard who opined that the difference between the numbers of men and women pursuing the natural sciences at the highest level might be due rather to predilection and intellectual inclination than to sexism. Again we are dealing with a bland truism; but the long knives came out, and Summers was dispatched.

This etiquette is related to the cry for "safe spaces," as college students, a majority of them female, demand to be protected from ideas and utterances that somehow, as they claim, deny their very existence or would cast doubt upon what they claim are their incontestable experiences as members of some historically underprivileged group. Their critics laugh at them and say that such students, "snowflakes," want to lock our colleges into an orthodoxy that is unenlightened and medieval. These critics are wrong in their diagnosis and inaccurate in their criticism. Anyone who knows a thing about the medieval university knows that it was less like a tidy little garden than like a jungle or a jousting arena, less like a cottage industry producing dainty flower arrangements for a formal table than like a foundry, with much sweat and noise, with the man-intensified flames fired hot enough to separate ore from dross so that falsehood could be scummed away. Thomas Aquinas, it has been justly observed, would typically put his *opponents'* arguments in a more powerful form than they themselves could do, so that that ox of a man and titan of intellect could wrestle them down, not by a loud mouth and easy public ridicule, but by the sheer mountainous power of calm reason.

It is also something of a mistake to point at the students and laugh at them for being weaklings. The students hold the hammer, and they know it. Yes, it is true that mere teenage boys in decades past—lads who stormed the bluffs of Normandy, sailed on ships cutting through the ice of the Northwest Passage, and slashed their way with explorers through the fever swamps and forests of Borneo—would not be preoccupied with hurtful words, and that a "trigger warning" in those days was the clutch of a rifle being loaded. But in our world of inversions, power is granted to people who claim that they have no power and who resent the greatness of their own forebears. They do not seek "safety." They seek to destroy. The strong man is bound and gagged, and the pistol is pointed at his head—the seat of reason itself.

In such a world, it is insufficient to say that higher education suffers. Except in the most technical of disciplines, and perhaps even in those, the very possibility of higher education comes to an abrupt halt. If a professor must negotiate an emotional and verbal and political mine field before he opens his mouth, then he is no professor any longer. He is a servile functionary, no matter his title and no matter how well he is paid. He instructs his students not in freedom but in his own servility. That many of the students demand this servility of him and of themselves makes their capitulation all the worse.

We must face the reality before us. The motto of my employer, Providence College, as of Harvard University, is *Veritas*: "Truth." One may examine the mottoes of one great college after another to see what people of old thought higher education was about and to consider how unthinkable it would be for any college to adopt such mottoes now. It is not so much that the colleges have failed to live up to them. We seldom live up to our ideals. It is rather that the colleges have repudiated them. Consider the mottoes of the Poison Ivy League schools alone. Dartmouth:

Vox clamantis in deserto: "The voice of one crying in the wilderness." It is doubtful whether one student in twenty at Dartmouth would be able to read the motto and know to what it refers: the self-identification of John the Baptist, citing the prophet Isaiah, and implying the rest of the biblical verse from which it was taken, "Prepare ye the way of the Lord." Is that what Dartmouth is about? The motto of Columbia: *In lumine tuo videbimus lumen*: "By thy light, we see light." Which young man at Columbia in the nineteenth century would not have recognized the words of the psalmist and appreciated their application to the intellectual life? The motto affirms that the worship of God, far from being an impediment to vision, enhances it; prepares the soul for receiving it; gives us the strength for plunging farther and farther into truth. The motto of my alma mater, Princeton, is *Dei sub numine viget*: "Under the power of God she thrives." They could keep that motto intact by substituting for God any number of appropriate genitives: *divitiarum* (riches), *potestatis* (power), *ambitionis* (ambition). Princeton does not thrive in the soft light of stained glass windows depicting scenes from the history of the Chosen People and the life of Christ. She thrives under the hard glare of glass and steel and concrete monuments to the pursuit of wealth and power.

The old mottoes assumed the existence of God, the moral law, and the beauty of pursuing truth. It is beyond the scope of my essay here to argue the unity of the transcendentals, though I do assert that even a skeptic must find it powerfully suggestive to notice that the secularization of the colleges has been accompanied by a contemptuous denial of the very existence of beauty and by lassitude in the search for truth except as regards that narrow range of truths that can be reduced to the residue of a test tube or expressed in a neat mathematical equation. When you say that what is considered "good" is merely what the politically powerful call good for their own purposes, or that what is considered "beautiful" is merely the result of subrational neurological tics and spasms, you do not merely put obstacles in the path of the young mind. You kill the search for truth in the egg. If there is no truth to be learned from reading Homer, then why bother, except as an archaeological curiosity? If the lesson to be learned from Virgil is the same as that to be learned from the slogans of our time, why spend so much money and time struggling with the *Aeneid*? What is the point? And indeed professors and students now agree: there is not much of a point. If beauty is reducible to neural promptings, why bother to erect that scaffolding in the Sistine Chapel and lie on your back for months on end, with the paint dripping into your hair and eyes, yourself never farther than one moment of forgetfulness from falling to your death?

Walter Pater wrote that all art aspires to the condition of music. We might apply his words to the contemporary university and say that all knowledge aspires to the condition of an empirical experiment and its quantified results. That is what people now assume. Pater might have been correct in his assessment about art; I won't argue the matter here. But it is certainly *not true* that the methods for acquiring knowledge of the anatomy of a toad apply also to acquiring knowledge of things that are not toads, as, for one example, what is good and evil.

This is not to say, though, that the colleges have abandoned moral considerations utterly. Relativism is an unstable equilibrium—imagine a pyramid upside down, placed delicately upon its apex. It might make you break out into a cold sweat to stand in its shade. The question is not whether some moral vision will prevail, but *which* moral vision. The colleges are thus committed to a moral inversion. High and noble virtues, especially those that require moral courage, are mocked: gallantry in wartime, sexual purity, scrupulous honesty and plain dealing, piety, and the willingness to subject your thoughts, experiences, and most treasured beliefs to the searching scrutiny of reason. What is valued then? Debauchery, perversion, contempt for your supposedly benighted ancestors, lazy agnosticism, easy and costless pacifism, political maneuvering, and an enforcement of a new orthodoxy that in denying rational analysis seeks to render itself immune to criticism. You sink yourself in debt to discover that your sons and daughters have been severed from their faith, their morals, and their reason. Whorehouses and mental wards would be much cheaper. They might well be healthier, too.

The rule that men are united only from above and not from below— by their common admiration for what is great and good, most gloriously and movingly manifest in their common worship of God, and not by the pursuit of creature comforts or power or wealth—implies that our colleges and universities are so only in name, not in reality. There is very little that is *collegial* about the modern college, nor does it require attendance at a faculty senate meeting or a faculty hanging to notice it. What *binds* the professors to one another, to their forebears, and to their students? To what beyond himself is each professor devoted? It is a hall of mirrors, everyone looking at himself and eyeing everyone else askance. God forbid I should ever wish upon students the amity that characterizes the relations between their professors.

And what makes it a *university*? What is the truth that bears upon every one of the disciplines? What do the professors understand as the relationship between the reading of a poem by Chaucer and mapping the stars in the heavens? The university is not a university but what my friend the theologian Reinhard Hütter calls a secular polytechnicum. People occupy the same area, and many thousands of them, but they are essentially severed from one another and from the past. It is a sprawling institutional development, without a center or a heart: a non-city, a non-borough, a non-village.

Such a place can be burdened with a stifling and immensely expensive bureaucracy and yet enjoy no intellectual or moral order. Hence the proliferation of silly courses, especially in what is left of the humanities: courses in Polynesian transvestites or the latent colonialism of Jane Austen (so latent that no sensible reader for nearly two centuries even suspected its existence). When I was a student at Princeton, the most popular course on campus was the freshman course in Shakespeare, taught by a brilliant actor and professor, Daniel Seltzer. That course has been supplanted by one in Young Adult Fiction—basically guerillas, vampires, sluts, and suicides—a course with a greater enrollment than all other English courses in its semester combined. When Longfellow was translating Dante at Harvard, people took for granted that you did not need to study the literature of your own language: that would be like studying the cuisine of your table at home. The plays of Shakespeare were what anyone with a good mind enjoyed and loved without having to be taught about it beyond the early years in school. Professors and students alike assumed that there was an order to higher learning: so at Harvard you would be immersed in the great literature of the ancient world, in Latin and Greek. From that promontory you could survey the rest of Western arts and letters. That assumption no longer holds. So you spend thousands of dollars for a course in teenage dystopias. From that little puddle or ditch you can survey exactly nothing.

What to Do

Some of the old colleges and universities can be injected with shots of sanity and truth-seeking, and those shots should be administered whenever possible. That is not a matter of healing a gangrenous limb here or there, but of searching the field of battle after a devastating defeat, and finding the few people still breathing who can be saved. So there are programs in Catholic studies at formerly Catholic colleges, or programs in Western civilization, or in the so-called great books, at colleges where the only people who did not know anything about Shakespeare or Milton were day laborers or immigrants still learning English, rather than tenured professors, administrators, accreditors, and trustees.

Sometimes we can put their ignorance to good use, for many people are so far past hating Milton for what he says about God and man, about marriage and sanctity, about liberty and virtue, they neither know nor much care what he says. We may then be like people administering antibiotics to heal the wounded, when the conquering army has forgotten what an antibiotic is, as they smile upon us for our foolishness in believing there is any special potency in a drug, as long as lice and dirty bandages and open sewers are doing their good work roundabout. What can be the harm in penicillin? Why should we worry if someone does the old-fashioned thing and learns about Dante?

Then there are those for whom "diversity" is not a slogan for cleaning and sharpening a pedagogical guillotine but a real value in itself. These are the rather rare agnostics "in the middle of the journey of our life," not contented with the dark woods but knowing nothing else, who suspect that if they are ever to get clear of it, they must at least entertain a wide range of points of view. These people are our qualified allies. They will look cross-eyed at administrators who on Monday cry "diversity, diversity" but on Tuesday write curricular guidelines that goose-step through Berlin in self-satisfied conformity. Why then *not* offer a real program in the development of Western civilization for those students who want to pursue those lines of inquiry? These are professors who can pretend not to know that the real object of a university education these days is not truth but power; and they can sometimes compel their politicizing fellows to pretend not to know it, too. We should consider that an hour spent reading Wordsworth can cure you of wanting to spend twenty hours reading contemporary inanities; as a single powerful experience of beauty, say the sensitive study of Botticelli's "Madonna of the Pomegranate," may make it hard for you to take seriously a "performance artist" smearing chocolate on her naked body. I tell my students that if they ever find me walking down the street reciting Welsh poetry, they may throw an odd look my way, but they needn't worry about it, because it will still be within the bounds of possibility. But if they ever see me entering a modern sculpture museum, they should call the paramedics immediately, because I will clearly have lost my mind.

I should stipulate, here, that such programs should not be infested with professors who despise the material they are to teach. It is telling that I should have to say such a thing. For great art is human in this regard too: it does not give up its profoundest secrets except to those who love. Hatred clouds the eyes and hardens the heart. I do not like the Enlightenment, and I have my reasons; therefore I am not the ideal person to introduce students to Hume and Kant. Some people seem to believe that the only way to teach about Western civilization is as an exercise in self-loathing. Such people are not really critics—because the true critic still must love. You cannot have anything interesting to say about Racine and classical French tragedy if its severe moral analysis leaves you cold. Doctor Johnson loved Shakespeare immensely, and that makes his criticism of the bard's pursuit of the "quibble," the groan-rousing play on words, all the more impressive and revealing. Love reveals. It is an eye, as Richard of Saint Victor says. No love: no vision.

Not Enough to Reform the Old

Ultimately, though, we must build new colleges. This is an absolute necessity. We have exemplars in our midst. Christendom College in Front Royal, Virginia, is a small school of about four hundred students, bravely and cheerfully Catholic and unapologetic in its commitment to the liberal arts. You cannot go to Christendom to study particle physics; that is one of the limitations of being a college and not a monstrous polytechnicum. The first time I visited Christendom, I was feeling some disaffection for the continual fight at my school, Providence, against those in the social sciences who wanted to destroy our Western civilization program. I thought that I would learn for the first time what a genuinely Catholic college was like. I did, but I learned something else too, something I never expected. I learned what a *college* is. What I mean is that such a school really is a common enterprise. There is a course of study shared by everyone. Professors and students eat lunch together every day, the same food, at the same tables, during an hour when no classes or appointments are scheduled. They hear the daily announcements together. They pray together—for classes are also not scheduled during the hour for daily Mass. If you go to Christendom, you are ushered into a genuine community in every sense of the word. People know one another, care for one another, laugh or quarrel or celebrate with one another, study the same thousands of years of history, art, poetry, philosophy, theology, and science, get to know one another's families, and set down roots in that humble place at the foot of the Blue Ridge Mountains. There is a ring of the sane and the salutary around it, and though every professor and student is a sinner, their eyes look to the hills *whence cometh their help.*

If all knowledge is one, and if the knowing subject, the human being, is one, then to have the intellectual equivalent of urban sprawl, wherein the teacher of poetry does not converse about history with the teacher of chemistry, but everyone is settled within his own little pigeonhole, is not to pursue knowledge at all, but only the *disjecta membra*, a finger here and a spleen there. The word *college* remains, but not the reality. Christendom provides the reality implied by the word.

Very different in some ways is another small school about fifty miles away: Patrick Henry College. The students there, almost all of them evangelical Christians who were taught at home for some or all of their youth, study the classics (either Latin or Greek is required), some of them going on to focus on the liberal arts, others on government. I have been to the school four times, and each time I have been astonished by the combination, in the students, of eager intelligence and innocent youth; their questions to me after my first lecture there (on a subject I chose for its being *out of the ordinary* for such students, namely, popular medieval drama performed to celebrate the triduum of Corpus Christi) were more perceptive and ranged more widely than any questions that any audience has ever asked me, including such audiences as were made up of professors at Princeton and Yale and other elite schools. "Dr. Esolen," said one young man, "what you say about culture here puts me in mind of what I have been reading in *Abandonment to Divine Providence* [the eighteenth-century Catholic devotional classic by the Jesuit Jean-Pierre de Caussade] about the sacrament of the present moment. Is that what you mean when you say that we need to recover our sense of wonder for the things about us now?" "Dr. Esolen," said one young woman, "you say that the Renaissance is ours to recover, but we often hear it said that the Renaissance was a period of renewed paganism. To what extent is it true that Christians can claim the Renaissance as their own?" And so it went on for nearly three solid hours.

There are other such new colleges or old colleges completely reformed, as it were founded anew, many of which I have visited: Benedictine College (Atchison, Kansas), The King's College (Manhattan), DeSales University (Center Valley, Pennsylvania), Houston Baptist University, the Torrey Honors Institute at Biola University (La Mirada, California), Saint Vincent College (Latrobe, Pennsylvania), Bryan College (Dayton, Tennessee), Franciscan University (Steubenville, Ohio), Our

Lady Seat of Wisdom (Barry's Bay, Ontario), Grove City College (Grove City, Pennsylvania), Hillsdale College (Hillsdale, Michigan), the University of Dallas, Catholic University of America (Washington, D.C.), the Great Texts program at Baylor University (Waco, Texas), and many more.

Such schools bear several distinguishing features. They tend to be small, so that young people are not ground to bits in the gear-teeth of a pedagogical machine. They tend to concentrate on the liberal arts, in a way that would now be called "classical." They attract students for whom ideas matter. Their faculty and students are like one another in their orientation towards the transcendent. They commonly pray together. The schools do not care overmuch about pedagogical fads. If you stay where you are on top of the mountain, everybody else, led down into the thickets and ravines by promises of cure-alls and new improved wisdom and toothpaste, will eventually, if they do not lose themselves utterly, be found clawing their way back to where you are, and will be astonished at your farsightedness. Trust in the Lord and you will not be confounded. Keep to the immemorial truths, what Russell Kirk called "the permanent things," and you will always be ahead of those with poor memories who seek after the timely and end up with the evanescent—like the spidery strands of a dream that melt in the light of day.

We need ten, twenty, thirty such schools for every one we have, and the same number of invasions of health into the pullulating swamps of those established schools that are beyond reform. This is not an airy dream. It is a dire necessity, an irrefragable demand.

How do we carry it out? Much of what I have said about our elementary and secondary schools applies here too. The most pressing need of most such schools is money. The true patriot does not send a check to Benedict Arnold, hoping that some of it will find its way back to Washington's army. You do not build a brothel in the hopes that some of the girls will learn chastity. The head of a drug cartel may want to build an orphanage to prop up his reputation as a pillar of the community. You do not help him pin up the streamers. Most of the Catholic and other Christian schools that have abandoned or betrayed their initial commitment to

Christ were literally built by the callused hands of men who never enjoyed the benefit of studying there, but those men believed in the aim, and the bricks of the buildings are mortared with their sweat. Such schools *have already cheated* their builders; they do not deserve another dime of support. Georgetown may schedule a Jesuit priest to walk across the campus once a day to secure the Catholic character of the school, in the same way that some cooks will dip a clam in and out of boiling water so they can call it chowder. They do so to fool the customers. Be fools no longer.

Thomas More College in New Hampshire—to name just one—needs and deserves your support. Your assistance there will increase and multiply in the good it does: it will assist in the miraculous grace of God, just as the apostles assisted in the multiplication of the loaves and fishes by doing what Jesus commanded and by holding the baskets for distributing the food. If you want young people who are on fire for the faith, who are attracted by what is beautiful in nature and in art, whose knowledge of the last four thousand years does not come from a politically correct lesson plan or the back of a cereal box, you must give them schools, professors, books, and dormitories, and those cost some money. Oh, much less than they cost at Land Grant State University or Saint Beelzebub's. The schools I have in mind are not encrusted with dozens of deans and hundreds of secretaries. They do not play the high-stakes roulette of college athletics (though in plain fact far *more of their students* will enjoy the human good of athletic competition, in club sports and intramurals). Unlike Harvard, they do not have endowments equal to the gross domestic product of many a nation. They do not have plumbing lines running from their treasuries to those of multinational corporations. They are—as youths and maidens themselves are—Mom and Pop operations. I mean it with no scorn. Better to resemble the Holy Family than the Roman legions.

Supposing then that we have the funds to hire teachers and gather books; and supposing also that we have the buildings to use, some of which, one might think, could come from disused rectories, convents, parish halls, orphanages, parochial schools, and monasteries. A couple of questions remain. How do we attract students? Whom do we hire to teach them, and how do we ensure that we will hire the right people?

I will answer the second question first. We are now in an age in which many thousands of people besides professors and deans can claim some acquaintance with a scholar's work and even his personal virtues. If you hire scholars who actually love and study Goethe, rather than squeezing Goethe's poetry, like liquid plastic, into the current political molds, other people not associated with the college can come to know about it.

We have yet to appreciate the nature and the extent of this change in cultural records. Who was the most foolish professor in the University of Paris during the years of Saint Thomas Aquinas and Saint Bonaventure? We do not know that there was anybody at all who could justly be called a fool, not even the brilliant and the brilliantly wrong theorist of the double truth, Siger of Brabant. But whoever he was, his own generation let him mercifully drop into silence, like a stone cast into a deep well. That is so no longer. Centuries from now, people who do not suffer our current psychoses will read about professors who gave their students credit for dressing in drag (Muhlenberg College), or who advised students that arguments against sexual perversion would not be admissible in class (Marquette University), or who elevated the trivialities of mass entertainment to the status of great art (everywhere), and shake their heads with dismay, using them as examples of how people can study themselves into a degree of stupidity for which Nature alone would never suffice. We do not produce many great comedians in the present. We produce a lot of material for comedians in the future.

So it will be easy enough to pick out the madman in the basement and the crazy lady with cats and tarot cards: I mean such people as form a prominent minority in most colleges now. It then remains to pick out the people who are sane and who have actually had what used to be considered a real education in arts and letters.

Finding them will not be so hard as you might suppose. Those colleges that have retained a classical education graduate plenty of students, and these tend to be superior as a group—because they are better educated, more broadly and deeply read, more conversant with a range of disciplines than are their counterparts in the schools of the lemming avant-garde. Many of these students go on to graduate school, knowing well that it may be hard for them to find more than one or two professors who will be glad to work with them. If after all of the snares laid in their paths they emerge with the doctorate, they are ready to be enrolled in the army of scholars who love the permanent things.

People in charge of new schools committed to a human education should follow the careers of these excellent students once they enroll in graduate programs. We should *know* who they are, where they are, what they are studying, and when they may be ready for tenure-track jobs. At other schools, where there might be two hundred applicants for a single job, search committees find themselves under an avalanche of unreadable papers, recommendation letters that say the same things again and again, predictable career patterns, conference presentations before an audience of six or seven, some of them awake, and utterly pompous cover letters that make one despair for the future of the professoriate. We can avoid most of the "noise" and the nonsense by pointedly appealing to established scholars who share our general vision of education, asking them to urge their best students to apply for an open position. We do not want to pick the best fish from a dragnet hauling hundreds in. That process does not really work, even for those who trust in it, as we should not. Once the obvious mismatches are tossed, the rest is a yank of the arm on the slot machine: a personal predilection here, a chance connection there, a paper actually read rather than nodded over, the working out of animosities among the members of the committee, and so forth. We want to encourage the best of our undergraduates by establishing a strong network of recommenders who will ensure them of a job somewhere, whether in a college or in one of our new classical high schools, when they have their master's or doctorate.

A caveat. Professors themselves are fit to evaluate a candidate's qualifications to teach in their discipline, the character of his writing, and his ability to engage students in a classroom. They are not to be trusted to consider the whole of a college's mission. Hiring cannot be left up to them, neither de jure nor de facto.

What Will We Build?

Let us never suppose that when we build a new college devoted to the permanent things, we will have something that resembles other colleges but with a different curriculum.

C. S. Lewis once wrote that all of economics and politics and education exists so that a couple of friends could chat about literature of an evening, smoking cigars and enjoying the fair weather. If we keep that in mind, maybe we can consider again not only what we teach and who teaches it, but how we teach, what it means to teach, and what it means to learn something.

And this is a great opportunity. A few decades ago, everyone was certain that the shopping mall with a hundred stores selling overpriced clothing was here to stay, and they built accordingly. Many of those malls are now empty, and grass is poking up through the cracks in their parking lots. A few decades ago, schools were built on the industrial model, as educational factories, and the word "homeschooling" had not been coined. Now the flat roofs of those factories are sagging and leaking rainwater, and two million children in the United States at this moment are learning at home. Another way to look at it is that progressives put their stock in technology rather than in Homer and Plato and have been crushed under their own wheels.

So let us take a look at what could be, because it has been or is now already here. I do not wish to prescribe a single pedagogical vision for all of the colleges we need to build. What would be the point of that?

First, the Integrated Humanities Program at the University of Kansas. Imagine a wide classroom with about a hundred students. Three professors are seated up front on a low stage: the English professors John Senior and Dennis Quinn and the history professor Frank Nelick. The men are all devout Roman Catholics, lovers of great literature and philosophy, art, and theology. They are dear friends. The course should not "work," according to current wisdom. It is not "student-centered." The professors do not even ask the students questions. Those are reserved for small group meetings or face-to-face discussions in the professor's office. Instead, the professors spend their time smoking cigarettes and *talking to one another* about the work in question, in the hearing of the students. Imagine overhearing a conversation, unfettered by political etiquette or by the constant need to pry answers out of your fellow students, between three learned men who enjoy one another's company and who are fascinated by *Othello* or *Paradise Lost* or Bach's *Saint Matthew Passion*?

Nascantur in admiratione: "Let them be born in wonder"—that was the motto of the program. I have seen it on the first page of a brochure that one of the freshmen received when he entered the program, long ago. There was Don Quixote on his skinny hack of a horse, Rocinante, holding his lance upright, and gazing upon the stars. That look toward the heavens was no mere piece of sentimentality. The professors, understanding that modern man has largely lost his connection with the natural world, would also take the students out under the night sky in Kansas to learn their way around the vault of heaven and name the stars above. They taught the students how to dance—that is, hand in hand, arm about the waist, not the jitters and spasms of an animal in the throes of a seizure. They taught them how to sing. They required that the students commit to memory many measures of that most exalted of the human arts—poetry.

The program was a tremendous success and soon attracted the envy and the enmity of much of the faculty. "What is happening to our hippies?" lamented an article in the *Kansas City Times*. For some of the young people were becoming learned, and many converted to the faith and even entered monasteries. Such a thing could not be permitted to continue. But during the decade it lasted, the Integrated Humanities Program brought forth into the world plenty of young souls born in wonder and ready to bring that wonder to others, whether their own students in school or college or their children. I have met or corresponded with many of the program's graduates. They all say that it was the best educational thing that ever happened to them; it changed their lives.

Such a thing could not now be established at Yale or Harvard, or at Penn State or Wisconsin. It is barely conceivable at old schools with a faint Christian flavor, such as Georgetown. We can have that program once again—we can build it.

If that is not to your taste, or if that does not quite fire your spirit, consider then what in some ways is its polar opposite. I mean here the kind of instruction that prevails at Thomas Aquinas College in California. My first visit to a class there was something of a shock. In front of a class I am a showman, but the professor of the philosophy class I sat in on retreated into the role of a moderator and observer. He threw out questions for discussion. "Aquinas says that the proper object of the sense of sight is color," he said. "What then is the proper object of vision, assuming that vision is not the same thing as eyesight, but is a product of the mind?" And then he fell silent.

Five consecutive seconds of dead air will suffice to kill a talk show on the radio. You cannot even watch a home decorating show on television without ancillary music-noise to prevent you from thinking. Young people now find old black and white movies dull, because they do not know how to think about a human face and its expressions, how to rest content in their glow. I confess that I am not comfortable with silence in the classroom. But there was silence, and for more than a few seconds.

The students were engaged in what is called "thought." They were not competing with one another to see who would come up with what they thought the professor was expecting. There was no such tension in the room. There was a kind of fullness, the peace that Augustine called "the tranquility of order." Then a student ventured a thought. "We need to specify the difference between eyesight and vision. The eye sees color, but the vision sees an object, a dog, a tree, whatever." More silence. Another student then, "But does the vision see *a dog*? Aristotle says that we abstract the form of a thing, the kind of thing that it is, from the individual things that we see. But which comes first?"

And the investigation went on like that, for a full hour, with the professor very occasionally asking a question to focus the discussion, to make a distinction, or to redirect attention. Sometimes the students would cite a particular page, and then everyone would turn to it. Some students spoke more frequently than others, but all of them spoke. Some were more "driven" by the question on the table than others, but all of them were engaged. We can have this too—we can build it.

At Benedictine College—a now-thriving school whose president was given plenary power to recover its Catholic and Christian identity lest it go bankrupt—students enjoy wholesome big-band and ballroom and folk dances *every week*. All we need is a big room or two and the musicians. We can have them. We can have science classes that actually go outdoors where students can see the world God made, or where they can plow the earth to plant corn. We can have students learn to sing four-part harmony. We can have weekly meetings to discuss books not on anyone's syllabus. Students at Patrick Henry College, at Thomas Aquinas College, and for all I know at many other new colleges in the liberal arts do much of the physical work that makes the college possible—the boys doing most of the groundskeeping. It gives them a deep personal stake in the college: as Michael Farris, the chancellor of Patrick Henry said in my hearing, it makes the college *theirs* in an intimate way. It gets into their muscles and bones. We can have that.

We can have literary clubs. We can have poetry readings—real poetry readings, readings of Milton and Herbert and Donne. We can have a course, taught by a biologist and a Thomist philosopher, on what it means to be an organism rather than a machine or an inanimate aggregate of matter. We can have a course on Shakespeare, taught by an actor and a theologian. We can have men's debate rooms. We can have women's choirs. We can have anything we please, things that used to be common in the world, but which now have ranged against them all the massed cannons of the large institutions, their professional habits, their prejudices, the narrow training of the professors, the fixities of credits and schedules and departmental curricula, the campus politics and turf wars, and the mighty inertia of a lumbering machine.

We can have *people talking to one another* regularly about God and man. We can immerse ourselves in beauty. We can delight in the sweet company of the opposite sex. We can breach the barrier between students and the children of their professors. We can worship together and celebrate holidays together. We can create communities of friends who will remember one another as long as they live. It has been done before. We have done it before. We can build it again.

FIVE

REPUDIATING THE SEXUAL REVOLUTION:
Restoring Manhood

Modern man, as I have said, is weary of giving honor to the Father, the Son, and the Holy Spirit, so he falls back in his lassitude upon the three biggest things that are nearest to him, which he may worship without much exercise of his imagination. They are himself, his sexual passions, and the all-encompassing state he has built in order to prop up his rickety being and to liberate him sexually from all of the family-protecting and culture-forming restraints that used to humanize his brute impulses and channel them into noble deeds. He flogs a sluggish horse.

Esau came home ravenous from a day's hunting in the fields and traded his birthright to his two-seconds-younger brother, Jacob, for a "mess of pottage," a bowl of good hearty stew. At least Esau enjoyed the meal. His body profited by it, even if his soul did not. We have traded our birthright, and our children's birthrights, and sometimes the very lives of our children, not for a bowl of stew, but for a bowl of grass, sand, dead mice, toadstools, and glue, the whole foul mix lubricated with sex to make the venom go down.

Chesterton wrote that "the more modern type of reformer," encountering a fence across a road, "goes gaily up to it and says, 'I don't see the use of this; let us clear it away.' To which the more intelligent type of reformer will do well to answer: 'If you don't see the use of it, I certainly won't let you clear it away. Go away and think. Then, when you can come back and tell me that you *do* see the use of it, I may allow you to destroy it.'" Our customs regarding sex and the family have been battered down without anyone's caring about why they were there in the first place.

Let us remember what those customs were. The word "sex" itself suggests distinction, separation. Our public schools recognized the fact. You will therefore often see, sculpted in the concrete lintels of old school buildings, the words boys and girls over separate entries. For the boys and girls would line up with their own sex, and often be seated in class with their own sex, too. Boys and girls wore recognizably different clothing. They wore their hair differently. They engaged in different forms of play. When they learned to dance, they learned the "roles" for each sex and were not like sexless epileptics jerking and lurching across a dance floor, lewd yet without the touch of a human hand.

Their dances were chaperoned. They dressed up for them, not down. Boys were expected to take the initiative, except on the occasion invented by the fertile imagination of the cartoonist Al Capp, "Sadie Hawkins Day," when the girls got to ask the boys—a day, says the big handsome lout Li'l Abner, that strikes fear into the heart of every red-blooded American boy.

Sex education meant a week or so out of your health class, with the boys and girls separated, lest the instruction provide opportunity for embarrassment or crude jokes at the expense of some shy person of the opposite sex.

There were recognized "rules" regarding what was and what was not permissible to young people who were not married. I have seen a book for boys, written in the 1950s by a medical doctor who was no conservative, which flatly assumes that sex before marriage is a crime against the girl and is unworthy of a boy who wants to become a genuine man. The doctor says he disagrees with those who class masturbation as a moral evil, but he does agree that it blunts the young man's drive, it turns his attention narcissistically towards himself, and it shows a lapse of self-control. That was then the *liberal* view.

As late as the 1970s, pornography was called *dirty*. As late as the 1960s, many hotels would not give a room to an unmarried man and woman. People would not rent houses to such, either. This is now called "discrimination" against "cohabiters," but at that time it was a matter of common decency. If you got a girl pregnant, her brothers would show up at your door and congratulate you on your upcoming nuptials. Therefore you either did not get her pregnant in the first place or you agreed with the brothers, did the honorable thing by her and the child, and mended your ways.

Cosmopolitan used to be a family magazine. The rot had already begun, by the 1960s, to eat through America's moral timbers, but attorneys for the defense in *Griswold v. Connecticut* could still argue that a prohibition on contraceptive drugs protected the common good by preserving the most obvious deterrent against fornication. People still had a sense that the right thing to do was to preserve sexual intercourse for marriage, and many still did so. No one talked about a "rape culture" on college campuses, because there was not even a *fornication culture*, not yet. Colleges still had separate deans for the men and the women. Nobody ever conceived of the madness of mingling the sexes in army platoons. Even the feminists never argued that women should be perched atop fire engines.

All that is gone.

The levelers predicted a world of harmony and free love and no "hangups" and childlike delight in nature, especially the nature of naked human bodies. People who actually remembered that, as Shakespeare put it (and Shakespeare was no puritan), "the expense of spirit in a waste of shame / is lust in action," knew that none of that would come to pass. Their predictions were in error only insofar as they were not pessimistic enough.

Pope Paul VI, in the encyclical *Humanae Vitae,* predicted that woman would become the sexual plaything of man; he did not predict that plenty of women would ape the worst vices of their brothers and use men as playthings in turn. Paul consistently warned that contraception would lead to more, not fewer, children born out of wedlock; even he did not foresee the utter collapse of the family in vast regions of the West. Orthodox Catholics argued that to legalize abortion would naturally increase the numbers of abortions, rather than merely making safer for the mother the abortions that were already performed. Even they did not predict a million to a million and a half dead every year in the United States alone. The happy-preachers said that easy divorce would not increase the number of divorces but would only alleviate the pain of divorces that already were going to occur. Even they did not predict that from four to five out of ten marriages in the United States would end in divorce; and *nobody at all* foresaw what I would call the index of familial disruption, that is, the percentage of sexual liaisons of at least a year's duration that produce a child, whether or not it is allowed to live, and that end in failure. In fact, no one really knows what *that* evil number is. Marriage is in free-fall, and multitudes of ordinary people who in any healthy culture would be married and having a fine brood of children now live in a protracted adolescence or in loneliness and disillusionment.

Nobody foresaw the endless disintegration of sexual personality that is implied in the ever multiplying categories of "identities." Nobody foresaw that we would be throwing parades for perversion and sadism and recommending them to our children. Some people foresaw that it would be open season on girls. Nobody foresaw that it would be open season on boys, confusing them and corrupting them in their never-sure sense of developing masculinity.

Liberal Christians in 1966 could proffer the poor excuse that the experiment was untried, that they did not know any better, that Jesus did not really condemn sins of the flesh, and that the times they were a-changing. Christians fifty years later do not have even that excuse. The experiment has been an unmitigated disaster. Those fences? They were levees, not fences. The churches took down those levees and erected signs in their place, reading, "Now, above all, be nice." The rain has come, the river has risen, it has broken down the few untended levees remaining and buried the pretty little signs under a hundred feet of mud, and water that once did productive work for mankind now spreads like a vast malarial marsh over what used to be fields and farms and villages, simmering and breeding vermin in the sun.

Christians must repudiate *the whole sexual revolution.* All of it. No keepsakes, no exceptions. Remember Lot's wife.

Let me spell out what that means, practically. I will try to focus upon the health we gain, rather than upon the false pleasures and false freedoms we give up. In this chapter I will consider the restoration of manhood, and in the next, the restoration of womanhood. Both are necessary, because you cannot corrupt one sex without corrupting the other. The seminal error of feminism, the worm gnawing away in the heart of it, is the assumption that you can actually seek the good of woman without taking account of the good of man, as if the sexes were independent of one another, or forever antagonistic. Man and woman are for one another.

Male and Female He Created Them

First let us establish that there are such things as the sexes.

Some critics say that the modern world is obsessed with sex. That is not true. The modern world is obsessed with excitations and with "identities." It has huddled itself into deliberate ignorance as regards sex. It is not puritanical about the beast with two backs. It is a veritable shrinking flower when it comes to actually *seeing* and appreciating the sexes for what they are.

I mean this quite literally. We are taught from the time we enter the indoctrination centers that *the only differences between men and women are trivial matters of plumbing.* It is not true.

When the European missionaries came to the New World to evangelize the natives, they did not find creatures of a different species. They found human beings, male and female. They did not find any tribes in which the women met in council, hunted the large animals, smoked the peace-pipe, trained up their daughters in savage displays of physical courage and endurance (the "sun dance" of the Plains Indians, for example), and established elaborate hierarchies of honor. They did not find any tribes in which the men took care of small children, gathered roots and berries, made themselves up with pretty decorations to delight their women, ground corn kernels to powder to make bread or paste, carried water while the women were singing war-songs, gossiped with one another to share the news and to keep daily morals in line, and made "nests," as it were, as clean and neat as possible, for the sake of the little ones, and because that is the way they liked things best.

They found men and women. That is what you will find wherever you go in the world.

I once saw a small child from India climbing half over the rails of a wooden bridge to spit into a creek and watch it go. Of course the child was a boy. Reverse the sexes in any common social situation and consider how many milliseconds it takes before the experiment collapses into caricature or absurdity. The wives are playing chess while the husbands are having tea and scones. Really? The girls are playing poker while the boys are talking about the kinds of flowers they are planting in the kitchen garden. Really? A woman greets her friend, whom she has not seen in five years, with, "Laurie, marriage *must* be doing good for you—you've put on forty pounds since I last saw you!" Really? A man wakes up in the middle of the night and hears some strange noises downstairs. He nudges his wife and says, "Honey, I hear something in the basement—would you go check it out?" Really?

A teenage girl says to a female professor that she doesn't believe in God, but rather in science, the Big Bang. The professor laughs at her and says that she's an idiot, ignorant of both science and religion. The girl laughs in turn and feels proud to have been ridiculed. Really? A girl learns how to box and pummels the girl who has been bullying her in the schoolyard, and this forms the basis of an enduring friendship. Really?

The ways of men and women take different forms in different places and at different times, but they are always and immediately recognizable as the ways of men and the ways of women; they are as recognizable as smiles, frowns, laughter, and other gestures that are universally human. We know Helen of Troy—gracious, charming, intelligent, scheming, dangerous, utterly beautiful, with a tender conscience but not too tender, either. Helen still lives among us. We know her sister Clytemnestra— regal, imposing, calculating, passionate, furious, contemptuous of men who do not live up to her expectations, motherly, and implacable. Clytemnestra still lives among us. We know Rosalind—girlish, sprightly, self-aware, cheerful, capable of utter loyalty and head over heels in love. Rosalind still lives among us. Mr. Micawber and Mrs. Micawber, Antony and Cleopatra, Romeo and Juliet, Tristan and Isolde, Elizabeth Bennett and Mr. Darcy, Milton's Adam and Eve, Anna Karenina and Vronsky, Dmitri Karamazov and Grushenka—we know them all, and there is no reason why we should pretend that we do not. As for their being what is called "socially constructed"—that every single one of the thousand or two thousand cultures whereof we have any evidence or experience should all line up, with the same kinds of things manifest in the behavior of men and women, all as it were by random chance, by accident; cultures independent of one another and in every climate and at every stage of technological development; hunter-gatherers, shepherds, farmers, warriors, fishermen; *that* is as incredible as to believe that you could balance the Empire State Building on its spire, with all the countering forces miraculously lining up to keep it stable. No, our customs are rather established upon the firm and unchanging basis of human nature.

Men and women are different from one another, down to the roots— down to the cells. We have merely trained ourselves not to see it or not to admit it when we see it. It is a willed stupidity. It is also a willed grimness, a willed refusal to delight in the natures God has given us. There is nothing glad or merry about it.

Let Boys Be Boys

Sexual morality is predicated upon the reality of sexual being, male and female. The morality is inseparable from the reality. If there is no such thing, really, as male and female, only some convenient organs for reproduction, then there is no reason why "a man should leave his mother and father, and cleave unto his wife, and they two shall be one flesh." We have to recover a strong sense of the beauty of each, and of their essence as *being-for* the other; man is for woman, and woman is for man, and both are for God.

That means we must cease the destructive chatter about "gender roles," as if they were thoroughly arbitrary and not built upon nature. We must see past the factitious distinction between the natural and the social, because man is by nature a social being, and the societies he builds are predicated upon his nature. There is no human masculinity out there, free-floating in the space of ideals; it is always grounded upon the physical and psychological basis of the human male. Nor is there a physical human maleness that is not already oriented towards its social flourishing and fulfillment. A role is something we pick up as actors, and we can exchange one role for another. A man can act like a dog, but not very well, because in fact he is not a dog. A man can act like a woman, but not very well, because in fact he is not a woman. When a man is a man, he is not simply playing a role. He is fulfilling his being.

When we raise boys and girls, we raise them at once in accord with the sexual nature they possess already and with the flourishing of that nature that we hope to see as they become husbands and wives, fathers and mothers. We must always have that aim in mind. The boyishness of the boy is to come to flowering in manhood and fatherhood. The girlishness of the girl is to come to flowering in womanhood and motherhood. That is what the sexes are for. We want no longer to deny reality. We want to work in harmony with it, shoring up its weakness, confirming its strength, and delighting in its beauty.

What follows may sound harsh to our ears but would strike any people *other* than those scorched by the sexual revolution as mere common sense and charity. Any new social custom and any form of instruction that places a premium on girls' *pretending* to behave like boys, or vice-versa, is destructive. Pornography reduces masculinity and femininity to a few physical organs and their action, often their perverse action.

Man and woman in pornography do not unite; they rub. These cross-gender customs reduce masculinity and femininity as well, without the ugly obscenity, but therefore also without the admonitory stench of the obscene. Man and woman in these do not unite; they irritate. I am not saying that girls should never play ball and boys should never dance. I am saying: be wise. Take the fingers out of your ears and the palms from your eyes.

Boys have been especially hurt. A girl grows into womanhood more naturally than a boy grows into manhood, because the potential for motherhood is expressed so obviously in the form of her body; it cannot be missed. A girl who climbs trees with her brothers and plays ball will naturally and easily turn towards more womanly pursuits as those brothers surpass her in bulk and strength, and as her own body grows less fit for the boyish things. That is why female athletes sometimes take drugs to suppress the working of the natural hormones in their bodies; or the sports themselves suppress the hormones, as when female long distance runners lose so much of their natural fat that they no longer menstruate. Their bodies "judge" that they are not fit to conceive and bear and care for a child, exactly as if they were starving.

But the boy must be *made into* a man; nor is it true that, once he has established himself as a man, he need never worry about it again. Manhood is risky. It must be publicly affirmed, and you can lose that affirmation by cowardice or effeminacy. See the movie *Four Feathers*. See the old Western *Branded*. Which cultures have recognized these truths? *Every single one of them but ours.*

Consider the institutions that used to guide the boy's natural risk-taking towards healthy objects. The Young Men's Christian Association—is so no longer. The Boys' Club of America—is so no longer. The nineteenth-century Lyceum movement, for the intellectual development of young men—gone. The Boy Scouts of America now seem to believe that men who are sexually attracted to boys, men who *have not* negotiated the passage from boyhood to full manhood, ought to be scoutmasters. That is either insane or cruel or both, and it shows that, at least officially, the Boy Scouts do not believe there is such a thing as *boyhood* that is to become *manhood*. They do not know what boys *are,* or they pretend they do not. They might then be called the Physically Immature Male Scouts of America. Traitors.

Children, we say, have "energy" that adults no longer have, and nobody says that that is a "stereotype." It is plainly obvious. It is because of their metabolism and the needs of their growing bodies. That is why children run around. But the body of the boy is very different from that of the girl. Why then should we expect that the needs of those bodies will be exactly the same? The rough-housing that boys engage in unless they are forbidden it or unless it is smothered in them by drugs serves a variety of perfectly natural ends. If you gave girls a thousand years they would never invent football, for the simple reason that their bodies do not yearn for football. The boy's body does, or for something very like it. In a way that men themselves find impossible to explain, it feels good to tackle and to be tackled—to land with a hard thump to the ground, and to be sore all over for the next two days. It feels good; that is the body's signal that they should do that sort of thing. It builds, thickens, and hardens the bones.

Not all boys like football, of course. Some would like to roam the woods hunting for food, if there were woods, and if we did not live in a police state, where the natural is illegal and the perverse is protected and promoted. Some would like to get together with other boys to play musical instruments. The band of brothers is sometimes a band indeed. Some turn towards tools, the more powerful the better, to work with their hands and turn shapeless wood into things of use and beauty. Some would join one another on their backs, sliding underneath the chassis of a car to inspect the works, learning everything about how machines work. Why should we pretend that we do not know these things? Women sew, but men invent the sewing machine. Or they would—if we encouraged them to be themselves and gave them the space for it, without the distractions of the opposite sex nearby. The boy must leave his mother, the human being he loves most in the world, in order that he might return a man, one who can be to another woman what his father has been to his mother. All truly loving mothers want this for their sons. They want them to be strong and tall and manly, in soul as well as body.

No Girls Allowed?

Therefore we must say, "Enough of the callous bigotry against normal boys!"

Why do boys form gangs? Because it is natural for them to do so. They will form them either for innocent and healthy things or for thrills and destruction. The boys who organize themselves in a "secret" club and hang a sign on the door, "No Girls Allowed," are simply doing what all boys in all cultures do, in one way or another. It is not because they don't like girls. How can we be so dense as not to see the reason? It is precisely because *they are* attracted to girls that their nature requires them to keep the girls away, for a time.

For what purpose? Consider the long period of sexual latency that in sane times shielded a child from the fire and fury of desire. Those many years of latency, that blessed time of *not having to compete for mates,* gives the child the breathing space to be a child and to learn the thousand things he or she needs to learn before the body reaches adulthood. Girls, we know, mature more quickly than boys; they speak earlier, they attain to puberty earlier, and they are interested in boys earlier than boys are interested in girls. The boy's physical, psychological, and intellectual development is more protracted. A fifteen-year-old girl will have the body of a twenty-five-year-old woman. No fifteen-year-old boy has the body of a twenty-five-year-old man—they're not even close.

The boys-only clubs are a form of latency in one sense and a form of sexual and intellectual development in another. Boys sense that they cannot be themselves in the company of girls. More particularly, they do not form close friendships with one another in the company of girls. Boys who are shy or unathletic or slower to develop are hurt the most by the prohibition against this feature of normal boyhood, because the early grower, the tall boy, the athlete, will be admired no matter what; everyone else will be scorned or ignored. But when boys *are* alone, they work out a kind of natural hierarchy that gives everyone a place, and they establish *rules* that transcend them all and that unite them. Of course most such things have their comical side. We can recall the club that Tom Sawyer formed with the other boys in the cave along the Mississippi River. If any of the boys were to betray the club's secrets, the others would kill one of the members of his family. Unfortunately, Huck Finn didn't have any family to kill, and it looked as if he would have to be left out of the club, when all at once someone thought of a good substitute: they could kill the Widow Douglas, at whose home Huck was supposed to live. "Oh, that'll do!" cried the boys, with great relief—because they did like Huck a great deal.

Girls cannot know it except by report, but boys are actually kinder to one another when they are by themselves, even when they fight. When the girls are around, then they have to show off, they grow nervous and suspicious of one another, and they will try to win points with the girls by displays of dominance over their weaker fellows, a dominance that is accompanied not by grace, or by honoring the courage of a boy who lacks the stature and strength to win a fight, but by contempt and dismissal.

And after all, who are we to sneer at a natural human invention, and one that has proved throughout history to be immensely productive and conducive to the common good?

When Michelangelo was a boy, his father sent him to work and learn as an apprentice in the most successful atelier in Florence, that of the painter Domenico Ghirlandaio and his brothers. There the boy learned how to make paints of various hues, how to make and use different kinds of brush, how to prepare a wall for fresco, how to work while the plaster was still wet but not too wet, how to draw up "cartoons," literally big sheets of paper for drawing up the composition of the whole. These and a hundred other things, about which I who am no painter am ignorant, the boy had to learn, along with other boys of various ages, all of them supervised by the masters. This system, a development of the medieval guild, was to be found everywhere in Italy during the Renaissance, producing brilliant artists by the scores and excellent artists by the thousands. Its success has never been equaled.

Someone may say here, "But only think what those studios could have done had they admitted girls also!" That is not sane. It is always dangerous to speculate on what *would have been,* but it is perfectly mad to predicate a result that has never been found in the history of the world. We know that the Renaissance studios, as they were, gave us the Bellini brothers, the Della Robbia brothers, Masaccio and his followers, Fra Angelico, Fra Bartolomeo, Titian, Veronese, Giorgione, and hundreds more. The *thousandth best* artist working in Italy from the birth of Giotto in the late thirteenth century to the death of Guido Reni in the seventeenth would be renowned the world over were he alive now. We have the works to prove it. All art studios are co-educational now. So where is the Renaissance?

Or consider the Greek *gymnasion.* When Athenian boys turned seven they were sent to a largely open-air institution on the outskirts of the city for their instruction, both intellectual and physical. The Athenians and the citizens of the other Greek city-states relied not on numbers but on training, since none of the states was very large, and all of them together had but a fraction of the population of their perennial enemy, the Persian empire. The place was called a *gymnasion,* from the Greek word for "naked," because that's how the boys and youths and men exercised there. Of course, when you are naked, you cannot claim precedence over others because of your father's wealth or the rich clothes you wear. You are reduced as it were to the bare essentials. Greek democracy was thus born in the *gymnasion*; and there too we see the development of citizen-armies rather than armies of professional soldiers. Greek philosophy was born in the back-and-forth intellectual wrestling matches that the *gymnasia* provided space for, without that having been anyone's initial intention. The Greeks came to believe that being ashamed to be seen naked by another man was a sign that you were a barbarian—that is, you were to be pitied, because you did not enjoy the advantage of living in a free and self-governing city. They also concluded that it was the mark of a tyrant to want to keep men out of such groups.

Now, if the *gymnasia* had admitted girls and women—there would have been no *gymnasia* at all. The Greeks invented philosophy, systematic political thinking, research-based historiography, the drama, geometry, mathematical proof, and democratic institutions; their achievements in sculpture and architecture would not be equaled until the Christian Middle Ages and Renaissance. Archimedes came within a whisker of inventing the calculus, two thousand years before Newton and Leibniz. The Greeks solved maddeningly intricate equations *without the use of numerals*, which had yet to be imported from India. Aeschylus and Sophocles cede pride of place as dramatists only to Shakespeare, and there are people who will rank them as his equals or his superiors. Homer cedes pride of place as a poet only to Shakespeare and Dante, who "divide the world between them," as T. S. Eliot said; but there are plenty of people who still rank Homer as the most magnificent.

What would they have accomplished if they did not distinguish between boys and girls? I don't know. I don't believe they would have survived long enough against the Persians for us to find out. But what they did *worked stupendously*. Does what we do now succeed as well?

A final objection. "But we have to think of equality!" To which I respond, "Equality in what regard, and why?" If it means that we deny boys what they need and what would cause them to thrive and, sometimes, to become a Phidias or a Caravaggio or an Aristotle, just because we do not want the resulting inequality, I say that that would itself be a gross inequity, the deliberate denial to someone of *what he is due*. It would be as if we were to feed our children not equally according to what their bodies require, but equally according to a calorie count, which would either starve the boys or fatten the girls. Besides, is not the rare Thomas Aquinas a gift *to all human beings, male and female*? Would the world really be a better place if there were no painting better than that of the greatest woman painter (Mary Cassatt, who indeed is a great artist), no poetry better than that of the greatest woman poet (Emily Dickinson or Sappho), and no philosophy more searching than that of the greatest woman philosopher (Simone Weil, perhaps)? Why should we not receive these things with gratitude, *especially since almost none of us, male or female, can attain them*?

Human beings should not be served up to a minotaur. Ideology is a minotaur. It parades itself as intellectual, but it is really mostly a beast hungry for power and for victims. Slay the minotaur. I believe in the equal dignity of every human being in the sight of God. I believe also in justice. An enforced and unnatural equalizing of people is deeply unjust. Give me Michelangelo instead.

I am not saying that *everybody* has to be an apprentice of Ghirlandaio or a student of Albert of Cologne or Socrates. But no one? We had guilds and schools for boys before, and not so long ago, either. They have been pulverized. Build them anew, and do so without apology. There are still sixty or seventy women's colleges in the nation, and every one of them receives plenty of federal money. There is nothing evil or strange about what was the educational norm for centuries. Learn from the past. The wheel was a fine invention. Use it.

The Necessity of Patriarchy

We train boys to be men. If you believe that the Church, the nation, and what is left of Western culture and civilization can be revived or rebuilt without the leadership of men, I suggest that you take an honest look at what happens when men retreat from the public square. You do not get rule by women. You get anarchy—social chaos that requires the vast machinery of state control to manage, control that enters into a host-parasite relationship with the chaos itself, much to the destruction of true liberty and the flourishing of communities.

Why is this so? All we have to do to see why is to rub the self-administered paste from our eyes. Men are bigger, stronger, more aggressive, and more tolerant of violence than women are. That is a plain fact. Foolish social scientists often look for esoteric explanations for violence. They miss the explanation that is nearest of all. Violence is fun. It makes things happen.

If you do not raise men to be fathers—not just progenitors of children, but *fathers* in the full sense implied by a phrase like "city fathers"— they will not therefore become compliant and gentle mothers. They will either drag out their days in ennui and desperation or go very bad, very fast. Nor will they lack for women, and plenty of them too, who will be attracted to the dangerous man, the rebel, the leader of the gang. The alternative to rule by fathers, which is what *patriarchy* means, is male domination in the form of a police state or in the persons of men outside the law.

Evidence is everywhere. We are told by our cultural "betters" that the 1950s were years of repression and false cheerfulness. Well, in that culture of repression people were free to leave their keys in the ignition of the car, to leave their doors unlocked at night, to let their children range all over town without supervision, to have shooting clubs in the public schools, to leave bicycles outside of a store without worrying that they would be pinched, to ride in the back of a pickup truck without getting stopped by the police, to tell children to get out of the house and stay out till suppertime, to have those kids walk a mile or two to school and back every day without worrying about kidnappers or perverts, to call on their neighbors (whose names they knew) when they needed some sugar or flour or when they wanted to play cards, to send their children to a parochial school without paying any tuition, to show up at a movie theater or a bowling alley at nine years old without arousing suspicion, to belong to men's clubs and women's clubs (whereof there were plenty to choose from) without being accused of hate or bigotry; and so forth. Oh, they were not saints, and their treatment of blacks was shameful, as they knew, and they did address that—the grownups, that is, and not their children, who took most of the credit for the civil rights movement, even though most of them in the sixties were still worrying more about acne than about social justice.

Such was the freedom they enjoyed, because *families* were intact, and families were intact and were everywhere because that is what happens when patriarchy (not brute male domination) is the rule. Liberty is to be measured not by what the law permits you to do, but by—to use a whimsical criterion—how far from your house you feel comfortable allowing your child to play. These days I often see a line of cars, with women usually behind the wheel, waiting at the bus stop near my house to pick up their children so that they do not have to walk the few hundred yards home. Or rather liberty is to be measured not by whether you are allowed to cast a vote for the candidate who you believe will best be able to deal with A, B, C, to Z, then A2, B2, C2, and so forth, but by the range of things that will not be in the province of the politician at all, because you yourselves, in your families, your local businesses, your local schools, your local beneficent societies, and your churches will deal with them quite well and in your own way, thank you.

Feminists have persuaded us to consider patriarchy to be evil and brutish, but wherever men retreat from leadership of their families and of their communities, things begin to fall apart. Once the boy sees that he is much stronger than his mother, once he sees that he can shrug when she shouts and nothing will happen to him, all bets are off; he needs the strength of the father to command his respect for his mother. What is the single condition of a boy's life that correlates most strongly with whether he will turn criminal? Not income, not by a long shot. It is whether he grew up in the same home with his father. Our prisons are full to bursting with fatherless boys who never became the men and fathers that God meant them to be. The collapse of the black family has been most catastrophic, and what is the result? What anyone not befuddled with feminist ideology would have predicted, from simple observation of nature and from the universal testimony of human cultures. One out of every three black men between the ages of twenty and thirty will spend time in prison. If we blame that on racism, then we had better explain why, in the days when blacks could not ride on certain seats in the bus and could not even play major league baseball, nowhere near as many of their men were in prison. Family, first and last—the family is where you learn of God and man, good and evil, courtesy, diligence, honor, chastity, self-restraint, and true courage. Give me poverty and the family as strong as iron and in one generation in America my family will be poor no longer. That is not speculation or boasting. It is the experience of millions of immigrants who came to the United States with nothing in their pockets, but with a great fund of moral capital; with faith in God, and firm loyalty to the family.

The Triumph of Brotherhood

The anthropologist Lionel Tiger, in *Men in Groups*, earned the wrath of feminists when he suggested that men had been primed by the exigencies of the hunt to form hierarchically organized groups, with each man performing a particular task, all of it coordinated in a team movement to bring down the mammoth or the wild boar. Some feminists countered by saying that women too had to form groups in order to locate and gather berries, which was a strange way of proving Tiger's point. Berries do not run forty miles an hour. Berries do not have antlers, hooves, or fangs.

Whether Tiger was right about the prehistoric cause, I will not venture to say. I do believe that his assessment of masculine nature was deeply penetrating. Look at the behavior of a football team. You have there the simultaneous and coordinated movements of eleven men, each of them with a task to perform that contributes its essential part to the success of the whole, and each of them submitting himself to orders from above; from the quarterback or the middle linebacker, who in turn has received instructions from the offensive or defensive coordinator, and ultimately from the head coach. A player who bucks the instructions will be disciplined, not in the first instance by the head coach, but by his brothers in the huddle. *The rules* take precedence, or there is no team.

Feminists, of course, fear and loathe this phenomenon, but without it we would still be living hand to mouth, if we had survived at all. Consider a couple of examples of what the band of brothers can do. Ancient Mesopotamia was one of the cradles of human civilization, fed by the grain grown on the plains between the Tigris and the Euphrates rivers. Idyllic? Not at all. The climate was harsh and punishing, and the rivers were prone to sudden and terrifically destructive floods, as was the Hwang Ho, "China's Sorrow," another site where civilization was born. The water from those rivers had to be used to nourish the land round about, rather than sweeping off the topsoil or soaking it and turning it into a swamp. That meant that the men had to construct systems of drainage, and since, far from their mouth in the Persian Gulf, the Tigris and Euphrates fall only about one foot over the course of fifty miles, the men had to coordinate activities on a large scale, and that meant that there had to be master architects, overseers, and small group leaders. Otherwise the task was impossible. You want to turn the small glens of short-summered Norway into arable land, when failure means that you perish over the long winter? You will not do it by egalitarian formlessness. Hierarchy fed the world.

It was the same thing on shipboard. You want the nourishing food that the sea can provide? That's well and good. But the sea is dangerous, and a sailing ship is a complicated machine, with its ropes and sails and spars and booms, and you never know when the weather is going to change. There is no such thing as a ship without hierarchy and instant and energetic obedience. You want to ride at your convenience on a bridge across the water? There is no building the Brooklyn Bridge without hierarchy. Have you seen the famous photograph of the workmen at lunch, hanging on a steel girder suspended hundreds of feet in the air? They are brothers. You want to trade your pottery and barrels of your olive oil for grain from Egypt? You will not get it done without hierarchy. Walk down your street. Whenever your eyes light upon something beyond the capacity of a single man to make—the poles stringing wires along which electricity flows at the pressure of a million volts—you are seeing the accomplishments of bands of brothers, organized hierarchically, and placing a premium on the virtue of prompt acknowledgment of authority. The alternatives are starvation, drowning, electrocution—or living hand to mouth.

The old universities themselves may be seen as the bold intellectual equivalents of ships, corps of engineers, hunting bands, linemen, football teams, and armies. The masons who built the universities with their hands were in this way very like the scholars who built them with their minds. We may add that the medieval universities had all organized themselves according to rules recognized all over Europe without there having to be any overarching juridical authority to enforce them, so that for the first time in the history of the world you could come from Uppsala, study in Cologne, earn your credentials as a doctor, and teach in Paris. The university was a hierarchically organized team of teams, itself possessing the form of a Gothic cathedral, a symphonic work of art composed of smaller, "lower" works of art, hierarchically organized. Hierarchy and obedience allow the lesser to partake of the grandeur and the authority of the higher, just as a dutiful son takes to his heart the wishes and the direction of his father, and learns to work alongside him, the younger man with the older man. It is revealing that when men boast about their fathers, they do not look to the old man's pliancy or even his mercy, but to his commands, and other men listen and understand and approve.

"So brotherhoods have been extraordinarily beneficial to mankind," someone may say, "but that does not mean that they have to remain as *brother*hoods." Yes and no. Our experience shows us that there is plenty of room for public activities in which men and women take part together. What it does not show is that the addition of women leaves the male group unaffected. This is something that only the men can speak about, because they alone have experienced the things to be compared. I have read an account of a Coast Guard ship whose captain was a woman, the only woman on board; and she said that the sex of the captain did not matter, because the spirit on board was the same one way or the other. There was of course no way she could know that, unless the men told her so, and most men will go far rather than to say anything even slightly critical to a woman for whom they feel affection.

We should also keep in mind that men are powerfully attracted to the brotherhood as such. That attraction is one of the three fundamental relationships of human society, along with those of mother and child, and husband and wife. When you admit girls to serve at the altar at Mass, you do not double the number of your servers. The boys lose interest, because something essential to what made the activity attractive in the first place is no longer there. Boys like girls in a very different way, obviously—in a way that will find its flourishing in marriage, and not in a team of hunters or builders.

So if men are to be men and not just male adults, we must revive brotherhoods: for inspiration, intellectual and moral nourishment, and fields of energetic and sometimes risky activity for the common good.

No apologies here. Surely people who say they value "diversity" need not blanch if all groups are not exactly the same!

Let brotherhoods then proliferate, and let the churches lead. Right now, men can congregate to get drunk and watch sports on television at a bar. Let them congregate instead to do adventurous work, the kind that stretches their muscles, physical, moral, and intellectual.

The Return of the Virtuous

Virtue, etymologically, means *manliness*, and I would like to specify what that means.

William Wycherley, a racy playwright of the Restoration era, gave the name of "Manly" to the hero of his play *The Plain Dealer*. Wycherley was no rigid moralist, but he took for granted that true men do not sneak, do not spread malicious gossip, and do not say one thing while intending another. They are plain dealers. I have heard Scott Rolen, whose name should someday be enshrined in the baseball Hall of Fame, say of his old coach Tony La Russa that if you asked him a question, you would get a straight answer, and it would be exactly what La Russa thought, no more and no less. The man understands that truth is more important than feelings.

In *Henry IV, Part 1*, the noble young Harry Percy, nicknamed Hotspur, indulges himself in a spree of angry talk against King Henry and will not even pause to listen to what his father Northumberland and his scheming uncle Worcester have to say to him. Finally Northumberland rebukes him:

> Why, what a wasp-tongue and impatient fool
> Art thou to break into this woman's mood,
> Tying thine ear to no tongue but thine own?

The man makes his words count, because talk is cheap. It is better to listen to a hundred words from your elders than to speak ten words of your own.

Henry James seems to have sensed the coming of our age more than a hundred years ago, as in *The Bostonians* he sets a disappointed young man from the defeated South, Basil Ransom, in an intellectual and emotional tussle with a bright girl named Verena Tarrant, who has been pushed forward as the great new light of the feminist revolution. Verena is beautiful, passionate, earnest, innocent, delightful, and naïve, and Ransom is in love with her. She believes that the advent of woman in public life will bring about such beauty and peace, it will seem to men as if Eden had come again. He knows that it is "humbug" but loves her none the less for that. Each one tries to convert the other to his or her way of thinking. Finally, at the crisis of the novel, Ransom says that, far from wanting to keep the other sex down, he wants to save his own.

"To save it from what?" she asks.

"From the most damnable feminization," says Ransom. What follows will strike the contemporary reader as harsh; that is my "trigger warning," and the very fact that we can use the phrase "trigger warning" without the most acute embarrassment tells quite a great deal about our retreat from reality. "The whole generation is womanized; the masculine tone is passing out of the world; it's a feminine, a nervous, hysterical, chattering, canting age of hollow phrases and false delicacy and exaggerated solicitudes and coddled sensibilities, which, if we don't look out, will usher in the reign of mediocrity, of the feeblest and flattest and the most pretentious that has ever been. The masculine character, the ability to dare and to endure, to know and yet not fear reality, to look the world in the face and take it for what it is—a very queer and partly very base mixture—that is what I want to preserve, or rather, as I may say, to recover; and I must tell you that I don't in the least care what becomes of you ladies while I make the attempt!"

We don't have to accept that note of exasperation at the end. A man does care very deeply what becomes of the ladies, and because he does, he must face reality, and not pretend that it can be what our tender feelings want it to be.

Henry James had not much of a Christian faith remaining to him, and that shut from his view the more exalted forms of manliness: the purity and passion of the best of Shakespeare's young men in love, such as Orlando in *As You Like It*, Florizel in *The Winter's Tale*, and Ferdinand in *The Tempest*. "I am yet / Unknown to woman," says Prince Malcolm to Macduff in *Macbeth*, adding that he has never forsworn himself, scarcely has coveted what was even his own, has never broken his promise, and "would not betray / The devil to his fellow." He concludes with a manly humility: "What I am truly / Is thine, and my poor country's to command." When the beautiful Perdita expresses some shame at being pranked up like a queen to celebrate her foster-father's sheep shearing, the prince Florizel, himself in disguise as a shepherd swain, reminds her that the gods themselves have taken on various shapes for the sake of love. "Their transformations," he says gallantly,

> Were never for a piece of beauty rarer;
> Nor in a way so chaste, since my desires
> Run not before mine honor, nor my lusts
> Burn hotter than my faith.

Well spoken. A true man, especially a Christian man, does not surrender himself to his base appetites. He does not define his manhood by how quickly he can get a girl into bed. He is not a muscled peacock prancing in front of a mirror. *That* is neither manly nor womanly but effeminate, regardless of where his sexual tastes incline.

"Quit ye like men," says Saint Paul, winding up his first letter to the Corinthians. That command is still in force. We must teach our sons and ourselves what that means, and hold ourselves to it, and form again the male groups that once gave manhood its direction and concentrated its energy. No excuses, no delay.

SIX

RESTORING WOMANHOOD:
Building Homes, Not Houses

The initial wave of feminists in the nineteenth century insisted upon a woman's rights as an individual—apart from her father, husband, or brother—chief among which was the right to vote. But long before that right was guaranteed by an amendment to the Constitution, women had been active in politics, if by that we mean not the holding of public office but speaking, exhorting, writing, and debating about issues that bear upon the common good. Many of the suffragettes were also leaders of the temperance movement, which aimed to shame men into giving up strong drink, so that exhausted and browbeaten miners, longshoremen, construction workers, and factory hands would not blow their meager pay on booze and take out their frustrations at home on their wives and children. Many American counties, bowing to their influence, were "dry" before the Volstead Act prohibited the sale of liquor nationally.

Pretty much everyone agrees now that Prohibition was ineffectual and a colossal mistake. They are wrong about the former and right about the latter, but for the wrong reasons. Most people who had drunk booze before the Volstead Act obeyed the law and refrained from drinking afterward or refrained from drinking nearly as much as they had before. Actuarial tables in the years following show a steep decline in alcohol-related deaths, leveling off after about a decade. The act enjoyed the support of leaders of both parties. Herbert Hoover called it a "noble experiment." But when, after about fifteen years, the noble experiment was terminated by another amendment to the Constitution, the whole nation breathed a sigh of relief.

What was wrong with Prohibition? It made illegal an activity which, though it can be abused, in itself is not wicked or destructive of the common good. In this sense Prohibition was *not* like ordinances prohibiting people from parading in the nude down the main street. Wine "gladdens the heart," says the psalmist, and Jesus at the wedding feast at Cana did not say to his mother, "Well, they should not be drinking anyway." He did not turn wine into water. Prohibition outlawed something that could readily be made by ordinary people in their homes; they could let apple juice hang out in the sun to turn it into hard cider. In this sense it was *not* like a ban on estrogen pills, which must be produced by chemists in a pharmaceutical factory. Prohibition turned what was essentially a local, domestic, and personal problem into a national concern; it nationalized what used to be called "public morals," which had always been assumed to be the responsibility of ordinary people in their towns, schools, businesses, and parishes.

"Don't make a federal case of it," we say when we feel that somebody is taking something far too seriously. Well, Prohibition made a federal case of drinking booze and then, by implication, even after its repeal, of every single other feature of human life.

We allowed politics to take over the home.

Carry Nation and her fellows wanted to pave a road from the hearth to the halls of Congress. But traffic on a road goes two ways, and government has armies and caravans of trucks and revenuers and officers with power that is difficult to check. The old saying "a man's home is his castle" never meant that the man had the go-ahead to bully everyone in his house. It recognized a zone of authority, exercised by men *and* women, that only in the most serious of cases could be overruled. A castle, after all, is a defensive fortification. In the castle, the father and mother govern *not* at the sufferance of political busybodies outside but by virtue of their own authority.

But the castle walls have been battered in, so that now, in Ontario, the head of the provincial education department can say, without embarrassment and without anyone's demanding her immediate resignation, that teachers are "co-parents." Who are those people in your living room, O modern woman? The tax man, the social worker, the principal, the policeman, and your children who understand the situation and know that you do not rule; they do. Where is your husband? His hands are tied—see, there he is, bound to the chair. Or he no longer cares. Or there never was a husband to begin with. Or there was, and the cad abandoned you. Or you abandoned him.

But the promise was great. Henry James, whose novel *The Bostonians* I have cited in the previous chapter, gives the reader a stunning example of the feminist oratory of his day, attractively packaged in the words of the sweet, earnest, intelligent, and very young Verena Tarrant. "Women," she says, "are simply the suppressed and wasted force, the precious sovereign remedy, of which society insanely deprives itself—the genius, the intelligence, the inspiration of women. It is dying, inch by inch, in the midst of old superstitions which it invokes in vain, and yet it has the elixir of life in its hands. Let it drink but a draught, and it will bloom once more."

There is an unstated premise here, that society had not in fact long been availing itself of "the genius, the intelligence, the inspiration of women." It had been, but not in the particular ways that Verena's handlers, especially the smothering, man-hating Olive Chancellor, had in mind. Verena means what she says, but James reminds us now and again that her father, Selah Tarrant, a self-styled progressive thinker, is only a cheap mesmerist and a charlatan. Verena is mesmerizing in effect, because of her beauty and innocence, but her words have all the breathless certainty of someone who has never encountered either physical or moral evil or been compelled to endure hard physical labor. Basil Ransom, the Confederate veteran who listens to her performance and is enthralled—not by the content, which he thinks is fatuous, but by her beauty—calls her a "hothouse plant," an apt description of the academic feminism plied by people who have no memory of fathers, uncles, and brothers crippling themselves with twenty or thirty years' cutting and hauling stone out of a quarry.

Verena winds up her performance with a promise born of genuine affection:

> Good gentlemen all, if I could make you believe how much brighter and fairer and sweeter the garden of life would be for you, if you would only let us help you to keep it in order! You would like so much better to walk there, and you would find grass and trees and flowers that would make you think you were in Eden. That is what I should like to press home to you, personally, individually—to give him the vision of the world as it hangs perpetually before me, redeemed, transfigured, by a new moral tone. There would be generosity, tenderness, sympathy, where there is now only brute force and sordid rivalry.

The twentieth century, bloodiest in man's sorry history, was soon aborning. I think we can safely say that Eve is a sinner just as Adam is, and that Eve's entering political life has not brought Eden down among us. It has done something else instead. I am not advocating any particular political program here but only describing what I see. Let me illustrate. In the movie *The Sound of Music,* Captain von Trapp, the widowed father of a large brood of children, is trying to teach the new governess, Maria, the different whistles to which each child is supposed to respond. When she asks what *his* signal is, he coughs and gives no response. The satire here depends upon a misplacement of virtues. The captain is actually a very good man, and he does love his children. But his nautical commands, essential on a ship, are absurdly out of place in a home, and in fact his children, despite his discipline, are unruly and unhappy. Maria must eventually set him straight: a home is not a destroyer.

Likewise, the law is not for your living room. It is not meant to cultivate the domestic virtues. It is not meant to adjudicate cases of hurt feelings. It is not meant to enforce an etiquette. It is not meant to put your children to bed at a decent hour. It is not meant to locate and punish "micro-aggressions." It is not meant to keep people from saying things that others do not want to hear. It is not even meant to see to it that everyone, regardless of behavior, receives a square meal.

It appears to me that our politics now reflects the worst of both sexes, not the best: the violent passions and ambitions of unscrupulous men and the shrillness and manipulative emotion-mongering of meddlesome women. Manliness and womanliness are hard to find. Congress is not an Eden but a nest of vipers. It is less likely now than a hundred years ago that a congressman will leap from his seat and cane his honorable colleague; but that did not often happen in the benighted old days anyway. It is far less likely now—nearly impossible—that two congressmen will engage in an all-out intellectual debate that results in real respect for one another and compromise or, better, a *tertium quid* that rises beyond the partial visions of either. Creative enmity is gone because, in the presence of woman, men become more intransigent, not less. And as for women and their ways of fighting, Kipling, thinking of the she-bear and her cubs, the cobra and her eggs, and women when they rise up in defense of their children, astutely pronounced, "The female of the species is more deadly than the male."

What Does It Mean to Be a Woman?

The answer is not "nothing."

I do not wish to prescribe a certain way of life for anyone. I am not saying that there should be no women doctors, professors, scientists, and lawyers. My sister is a physician, a specialist of extensive and grave responsibilities in one of the most populous states in the country. I work among women colleagues whom I esteem for their remarkable abilities.

My wife, who used to teach college courses in literature when our family needed the additional income, is a far more sensible and sensitive and intelligent critic than the great majority of professors of English.

The question remains. What does it mean to be a woman?

I hear the answer, mainly from a certain kind of woman, "It means whatever you want it to mean." Sorry, but that is equivalent to saying that it means nothing. Women, in my experience, prefer their nihilism to be dressed up in perky relativist clothing. Relativism is nihilism for girls.

If we are to believe the women's magazines on sale at groceries and drug stores, a woman is obsessed with her body, eager to learn new sex tricks, always on the watch for dirty revelations about pop-culture celebrities, prone to consulting horoscopes, ready to shell out a lot of money for new fashions, all-in for "safe" gay men who destroy one another's lives rather than women's lives, and firmly committed to "women's health," which depends on contraceptives and abortions and everything else that is meant not to restore healthy function to a diseased organ but to thwart the natural action of a healthy one.

If we are to take as evidence women's political shows, a woman is loud, vulgar, screeching, ignorant of history, morbidly touchy, vindictive, smug, voluble in slogans, impervious to the principles of any coherent political philosophy, and ready to see the world as the she-bear sees it when her cubs are restless and the food is scarce. Men, for their part, would be boorish, violent, indolent, reckless, cruel, proud, and ready to soak the world in blood for the sake of a principle.

That is not what *women* are. That is what *bad women* are. It is what happens when you fail to cultivate the difficult virtue of womanliness, just as the thug and the lout are what you get when you fail to cultivate the companion virtue, manliness.

Let me dispense with a common but empty objection here. We are told that to describe women or men as a group is to indulge in *stereotypes*. That is not to the point. The dog wags his tail and yelps for joy when his master comes home after being away for a couple of days. That is simply what dogs do. The three-year-old child pouts and cries when his mother tells him he can't have the candy he wants. That is simply what three-year-olds do. It is in their nature. Now, the field of activity for a human being, compared with that of a dog, is vast, making it difficult to predict precisely what he will do. But basic human nature allows us to foresee in a general way what people will probably do and how they will do it, or even how they will do what they are not likely to do.

The *character* of human beings remains constant, and this is why, as I have said, we immediately recognize men as men and women as women, throughout history, across cultures at all stages of technological development, and in all of the annals of literature. The goldfinch has a couple of diagnostic songs and twitters, and that is it. Human behavior is not so constricted, but human actions will always be recognizable as those of a human being, and the same thing goes for the subsets of men, women, and children. A flute player has an infinity of choices open to him, unlike the goldfinch, but whatever he plays, it will sound like the music of a flute, and not the music of a cello. It would be absurd to charge with "stereotyping" somebody who says that the flute is cheerful and sprightly. Of course the flute is cheerful and sprightly, and even if you play a haunting love song on it, the nature of the flute will color the song and make it very different from the same if you played it on the lugubrious cello.

Enough of that. Every culture recognizes the virtue of womanliness. What is it? What are some of its embodied forms?

"Cordelia, Cordelia! stay a little," cries the old King Lear over the body of his strangled daughter. His mind failing as he nears his own death, he thinks he hears her speaking: "What is't thou say'st? Her voice was ever soft, / Gentle and low, an excellent thing in woman." Oh, there are plenty of virtuous women in Shakespeare whose voices are not *soft, gentle and low*!—Beatrice is a spitfire, and Imogen has a streak of ferocity that can leave a crude and vicious suitor stammering. But Cordelia is indeed a gentle speaker, even when touched to the quick by wrong. She does not rail against her wicked sisters. She does not speak in anger against the father who has imposed on her words the worst construction. This softness does not imply weakness. She is firm in her commitment to the truth. At the opening of the play, she will not play the flatterer to her father as her hypocritical sisters, Goneril and Regan, do, using their glib tongues to gain his favor and ample shares of the kingdom he wishes to divide among the three daughters. "Unhappy that I am," she says, "I cannot heave my heart into my mouth." She is also firm in her love for her father, returning to England with armies from France when she hears of his ill treatment. "O dear father," she says, echoing the words of the boy Jesus in the temple, "it is thy business that I go about." But she is the "heavenly Cordelia," as the loyal Earl of Kent says. I don't believe that anybody ever called a young man, no matter how virtuous he was, "heavenly."

The gentleness of women, as compared with the roughness of their brothers, is marked upon their bodies in visible ways: hence Latin *mulier*, "woman," related to *mollis*, "soft," "tender." It seems obvious enough that when the woman is not defending her children, which she will do ferociously—so that a mother with poor judgment usually thinks that her children of either sex are in the right, while a father with poor judgment more typically thinks that his *sons* are in the wrong—it is of no advantage to the race that she be harsh and ungentle. We have in women the sex which for thousands and thousands of years has had to take care of the littlest and weakest among us. Women with a hankering for danger and violence may have sometimes survived their forays, but their babies and toddlers are not likely to have done so well.

Let us go to another scene in Shakespeare, from *As You Like It*. It is the court of Duke Frederick, who has usurped the rule from his elder brother, Duke Senior. His niece Rosalind has, however, remained at court, because she is the bosom friend of Frederick's daughter, Celia. Rosalind misses her father deeply, and Celia is trying to cheer her up, and generally succeeding, because Rosalind is a delightful girl with a naturally ebullient personality. Then one of the courtiers shows up to tell them that they are missing quite a sport. It is a wrestling competition, with the duke's champion, Charles, taking on all comers. Charles, says the courtier, has already broken three ribs of one contender, "so that there is little hope of life in him," and then served his two brothers just the same. "Yonder they lie, the poor old man, their father, making such pitiful dole over them that all the beholders take his part with weeping."

"Alas," Rosalind cries.

"This is the first time," says the court jester, Touchstone, "that ever I heard breaking of ribs was sport for ladies." Touchstone never lived to see women ushered into the front lines of battle to do obeisance to an egalitarian ideology and to give ambitious female officers a chance to climb the military's professional ladder, whatever the human cost might be.

In any case, the sport comes their way, and they see the next challenger, a handsome and tall young man named Orlando, ready to try his fortune with the champion. Orlando, his father dead and his elder brother having denied him a decent education, is, like Rosalind, a person without a place in the world. Rosalind and Celia beg him to stand down. He is embarrassed, as any young man would be, but he assures them that there can be no harm, because "if I be foiled, there is but one shamed that was never gracious; if killed, but one dead that is willing to be so. I shall do my friends no wrong, for I have none to lament me, the world no injury, for in it I have nothing; only in the world I fill up a place, which may be better supplied when I have made it empty."

This is the moment, I believe, when Rosalind falls in love. "The little strength I have," she says, "I would it were with you." And when, against all expectations, Orlando defeats Charles, Rosalind congratulates him heartily: "Sir, you have wrestled well, and overthrown / More than your enemies."

Rosalind is not a sentimentalist. She will later, in comical disguise as a boy, instruct Orlando, who also is head over heels in love with her, in all of the crazy ways of women—talking too much, being whimsical and unpredictable, running contrary to their husbands' moods, and so forth. We are meant to like her all the better for it. But when a woman like Rosalind falls in love, as she says, it is like the Bay of Portugal—no one can tell the bottom of it. Its origin is not Orlando's strength or his good looks, but his misfortune. *The woman has a heart for those who suffer.* She is compassionate, in the literal sense: she suffers with the suffering. She is like a bell that rings in sympathy with others.

Again we see the obvious advantages. The sex that bears and tends children *must respond* to their cries. This womanly sympathy, often manifest in real tears, is essentially personal and intimate. It flourishes best at the hearth, the bedside, the table. It is the passionate self-giving that makes the home. Abortion is a dagger twisted into the heart of a woman; and in order not to feel it, she must harden her heart in a way that men do not readily understand. *They* may view the matter with cold abstraction. That is both the strength and the weakness of the man. For the woman, the developing child is never an abstraction. Abstractions do not kick. It is why we find women working to take care of the children of other people, in day care asylums and elementary schools and in social work. The farther away from home and hearth such work is, however, the more problematic it becomes, so that now, with the virtue of sympathy run wild and careening far out of its proper sphere, children themselves have become the objects of national legislation, or rather its patients, the sufferers of policies that have the perverse general effect of undermining the family and ensuring that more and more children will be in need to begin with.

Which leads me to a third characteristic of women, out of the many that we could name. A man may build the house, but the woman makes the home. A man puts a roof over your head so that you can sleep without the rain soaking you or the cold biting your bones. You flop in a house. You *dwell* in a home. The old saying that charity begins at home is sometimes mistaken to mean that it *ends* there, if it ever begins at all. That's not the meaning. The home is the cradle wherein the child learns what love really is, and the mother and father also learn it—learn it by putting it into practice, giving of themselves for those small and weak and rarely very grateful creatures of their loins. A house is a wooden thing; a home is alive and warm. Home, not a house, says the gentle wife Mary in Frost's "The Death of the Hired Man," is "something you haven't to deserve." It is the first and foundational gift in any person's life, something we don't have to earn, as the old hired man, Silas, has to earn his keep and usually doesn't. Home is a human place. So Silas returns to a farm where he trusts that Mary and her husband might let him rest his head, preserve his dignity, and breathe his last.

For my money the man who thought most deeply about the home and how a good woman makes it so was Charles Dickens. In one way or another he is always thinking about *economics* in its literal and most human sense: the management of a household. *Bleak House* may best serve to illustrate the point. The heroine, Esther Summerson, a young woman with no family, is taken into Bleak House by her benefactor, the elderly Mr. Jarndyce. From the newly sunny Bleak House she brings charity and order to everyone with whom she has any dealing. By contrast, Mrs. Jellyby, who Dickens says practices "telescopic philanthropy" by taking up subscriptions for the natives of Borioboola-Gha, neglects her husband and their brood of children; her house is always in chaos, and it is no home. Mrs. Pardiggle, a sour pharisaical moralist, wrings sacrifices out of her children to show them off as she visits the poor, whom she angers with her high tone and her hard heart. Mrs. Jellyby and Mrs. Pardiggle—the one pleasant, daft, and unfeeling, the other harsh, sharp, and unfeeling—are, we might say, *professional* charity-mongers. Esther is the real giver of charity. She takes in a girl whose younger siblings have no support. She assists a street-boy dying of smallpox—and she contracts it from him, going temporarily blind. She knows what to say to soothe the sorrowing heart and when not to say anything at all. She brings light, and the best of it is that she is quite unaware that she does so. Esther Summerson's left hand does not know what her right hand is doing, yet everything she does is sensitive to the moods and needs of others. Esther is gentle but not to be moved from what is right, industrious but not exhausting to be near, soft-spoken but not mousy, delighted by the quirks of other people, saddened by their faults, trying always to interpret things for the best, yet not naïve, not easily fooled. She is an astute judge of character. She is exactly what any good man would want in a wife: like the beneficent sun in summer.

It is pointless to argue that these are *not* examples of womanly virtue. It is to engage in deliberate obfuscation to insist that men are sometimes gentle in their way too, as if that were to the point. Every single person alive in every spot on the globe knows such women as I have described. My readers can probably name three or four of them within the next ten seconds. Reality is what it is.

Rejecting the Way of the World

It was bad enough for the family when the Industrial Revolution took from the home its productive power and whisked the father off to the furnace blasts of a foundry for most of the day, six days a week. Then came the feminist movement, bidding to do the same with the mother. And make no mistake: what is now cloaked in the language of opportunity and civil rights was once openly advocated as an offensive against the home and the family. In *The Second Sex,* Simone de Beauvoir argued that an enlightened society would *prohibit* mothers from staying in the home to take care of their children. When Betty Friedan, a communist ideologue posing as an ordinary American wife and mother, wrote *The Feminine Mystique,* she did not argue that women did not have pretty much the same opportunities that men had for education and employment. She argued that despite those opportunities, women had been hoodwinked into believing that life at home was more fulfilling and were therefore bored out of their minds. The feminists in those days, as Midge Decter exposed them in 1972 in *The New Chastity and Other Arguments Against Women's Liberation* (which "new chastity" was not a virtue but a vice—living apart from those monsters called men), seemed to have a pathological loathing for the ordinary care of babies: "shit-work," as it was called by Shulamith Firestone, one of the bitterest and most deranged among them.

This is now the way of the world. If someone talks about "economic opportunities for women," he or she is not talking about the health and prosperity of the household, but about what money you make for yourself. Even the phrase "stay-at-home mom" is patronizing and faintly derogatory, like "stick-in-the-mud mom" or "sit-in-the-corner mom." Do we talk about a "chained-to-the-desk mom" or a "stuck-in-traffic mom" or a "languishing-in-meetings mom"? To do fifty things in one day for which you alone are responsible, for the immediate good of the people you love, is deemed easy, trivial, beneath the dignity of a rational person, but to push memoranda written in legal patois from one bureaucratic office to another, at great public expense and for no clear benefit to the common good, now *that* is the life. Chesterton put it well when he said that the work of a mother is not small but vast. A teacher would bring to fifty children the arithmetical rule of three, and though that is an interesting thing, it is but small and limited. The mother brings to one child the whole universe. That is no sentimentality. It is exactly true.

So let us remember our economics. Let us remember that all of our earning money is for the sake of the home. The home is not a flophouse where we stay and recuperate so that we can go back out and earn money, much of which we burn in the very earning of it, with eating out, no frugality, the extra car, the day care center, and so on. John Senior recommends a "gladsome poverty" as a remedy for the madness that subjects the home to the hamster treadmill—labor for the sake of labor, or worse, for the sake of prestige, for a desk and a title. We must say to ourselves, "We will not subject our children to the new thing in the world, having them spend vast tracts of their waking hours in the company of people who do not love them and who will not, a few years later, even remember their names. We will not hang our children by the ropes of our ambition or avarice. We will not institutionalize them at age three so that we may place them in a 'good school system,' that mythical beast, at age six. We will not mount the treadmill. We do not care what our 'betters' think. They have no great joy to show for all their sweat and grumbling."

Keep it always in mind. The world hates the family. The state is the family's enemy. The state grows by the family's failure, and the state has an interest in persuading people that the family can do nothing on its own. It hates fatherhood, and makes little pretense otherwise. It hates motherhood, though it makes a show of championing the unwed mother as well as the mother who, as the ugly phrase puts it, "has it all," though a moment's reflection should suffice to show that no one can give his or her all to a career *and* a family *and* the local community.

So what will build up in girls the family-heartening and community-strengthening virtues that we look for in women? What will give them that tenderness, the quick sympathy, the eye for what the weakest among us needs, that remarkable ability to do so wide an array of things for those she loves, rather than poring over a chessboard like an autistic savant, dead to the rest of the world?

Here I am painfully aware that I am a man attempting to speak to women about what women know best and love most deeply. I do not wish to emulate the folly of the modern woman who is wholly incurious about what inspires boys and what can lead them on toward a healthy and dynamic manhood. If men must raise boys to be men, and if only men really know how to do that, then I think the same can be said of girls and women. Allow me here merely to point out a few things I notice.

First, do not expect gentleness from young women brought up on the female form of pornography, the sleazy and mind-emptying "romance." Do not expect it from them if they are taught to swear like sailors, without the know-how and the risk to life and limb and the rough camaraderie that make the sailor's roughness pardonable. Do not expect it if they place before their eyes the glossy magazines that slash the soul like steel knives. Do not expect it if they are trained up in cat-fights. Every time you hear somebody whine about a "double standard," recall that we have many of those because the sexes are two, not one; and recall also that men treat cowards, seducers, liars, and traitors without the slightest mercy. A woman may weep in a department meeting and get her way; I myself have witnessed it. If a man does that, he loses the respect of his fellows forever, nor does he get what he wants. The other men scoff at him.

Second, you might ask exactly how it helps a girl when a parent, usually the father, presses her into competitive sports, when the team or platoon or ship's crew is not the pattern of female cooperation, when she knows that she will never be able to compete against her male counterparts at the same level, and when the development of her growing body is directed towards child-bearing, not towards loping across the savannah in pursuit of gazelle or hurling a harpoon to spear seals. Men and boys invent sports; it is an anthropological fact. We have had, for many decades, women competing in sports cordoned off for their sole participation, and while men and boys continue to invent games apace, women have not. They *could* be developing all kinds of beautiful and useful skills that would eventually bring sweetness and grace and health to their families and forge real social bonds among neighbors, but they are too busy learning to hit a softball in a field no bigger than the Little League stadium at Williamsport before a few other girls while the boys are off doing something else. What, ultimately, is the aim? Yes, there will always be tomboys, and I have no desire to tell girls that they should not be playing softball. I do desire to tell parents that they should not be *pushing* softball upon them.

Third, how can a girl become a woman like Dickens's Esther Summerson if she cannot do anything? Consider what a mass of contradictions we are. If a woman arranges flowers for a living, she earns our congratulations even if she doesn't do anything else either because she doesn't know how or because she is too busy at her flower shop. If a woman cooks fine Italian meals for a living—if her gnocchi, with their wonderful hundreds of calories, are famous all over town—we sing her praises, even if when she gets home she is spent. If a woman plays the violin for an orchestra or gives singing lessons, she can hope to find her name in the newspaper, even if she buys fast food for herself and her family on the way home from the music hall. But if a woman, because she is well versed in all of the household arts, *can do all these things* and in fact does them for the people she loves and for those whom she welcomes into her home (and she is not afraid of guests, because her home is always just a whisk or two away from hospitality), we shake our heads and say that she has wasted her talents. Not *developed them,* notice, and put them to use.

We must rid ourselves of the feminist spite that pretends to despise the woman of many talents and many tasks in the home, preferring the specialist who amputates and cauterizes and does one thing well, for herself primarily and sometimes even at the expense of the family. I said "pretends to despise" advisedly; *envies* would have been nearer the mark. Women themselves can testify to this; they know the looks they receive from a certain sort of woman as they mount the steps of the bus with three small children skipping along after. Imagine the most *human* place in your experience, the one that is warmest in heart and soul and mind.

It isn't an office, is it? We have plenty of second-rate men in our world. Our whole late capitalist bureaucratic human-resource drudging economy consumes second-rate men as fuel. We don't need any more. We need first-rate women.

What Is Life For, Anyway?

I am looking at one of my favorite paintings, "The Holy Family," by Bartolomé Esteban Murillo. It's a quiet and charming scene of domestic harmony. Joseph is seated, his carpenter's tools laid aside. He is wearing a handsome purple robe symbolic of his descent in the line of King David. Mary is seated to the left, glancing away from her work, winding wool into thread on a distaff. She has a gleam in her eye and a pleasant smile upon her lips. Joseph is holding the toddler Jesus by his hands, as Jesus, dressed in white, holds a small dove over his head, in plain sight of a little white dog. The dog looks up at Jesus with one paw raised, begging. A fine and homely allegory of Father, Son, and Holy Spirit, with the blessed Virgin looking on in her motherly care!

What is our life for? Why do we work? If Christians cannot remember the answers, then we are lost indeed. Work is not something you are supposed to balance against the claims of your family. Unless you are one of those few whose talents are required in a broad way for the common good of multitudes, if you are not working in the first instance for your family, then something is severely out of order. We live in comforts that the richest of aristocrats not very long ago could never have dreamed of, and yet we claim that we are too poor to have more than a child or two. The truth is the reverse: we are too rich to have more than a child or two, too committed to work for work's sake and to the purchase of prestige, mansions, the "best" schools, and toys for grown-ups.

Think now of the women you have known and loved. My mother's mother raised six children in poverty, her husband having suffered a nervous breakdown after fifteen years under the earth in the coal mines. She cooked, and her three daughters learned to do that too. She sewed, and so did her daughters. She had a garden. She tended first her bedridden father and then her half-mad and abusive father-in-law, also bedridden. She helped raise her nineteen grandchildren and a few of her great-grand-children. She was a devout woman who made no fuss and sang Italian lullabies to the babies. She was more energetic at age eighty, with a right arm made helpless with cancer, than most people are at forty. Should she have been pushing a mop in a hotel for a salary? I will remember till the day I die the very smell of the good things she cooked for us when I was a little boy—the fresh-cut potatoes roasting in the oven, the heavy coffee-and-raisin-and-stick-of-butter "boiled cake," moist and rich, the pies—endless pies—on holidays. I remember all of that with love, because it was offered with love.

My father-in-law's neighbor is a tart-tongued fellow who says that his welfare program is "You get up off your..." and so on. He is the head of a team of men who blast the bird guano off the undersides of the George Washington Bridge, then the Verrazano-Narrows Bridge, then the George Washington Bridge again, painting as they go along. Without such constant maintenance, one of those bridges would one day collapse, eaten away by the acids from underneath, and hundreds of people would plunge to their deaths. He is also handy around his home, which is well maintained, with a big yard for the growing family and two large dogs. Such work is *necessary*, and he is well remunerated for it. But his body will be shot by the time he is fifty. He knows why he does that extremely dangerous work: he does it for his family. Now then, not many of us do work that is absolutely necessary for civilization to exist, and those who do don't usually enjoy the most prestige. Farmers are absolutely necessary, as are quarrymen, miners, truckers, ranchers, construction workers, and people who maintain roads, waterways, bridges, railroads, and so forth. The rest of us earn a salary because we need to support ourselves and our families, and the work we do may be desirable, but is not absolutely necessary. My work is not necessary: we do not need teachers of English literature in the same way that we need farmers and men who maintain bridges. In fact, as I have mentioned, English courses in college are a little over a hundred years old, its having been taken for granted before then that you did not need special instruction to read poetry and novels written in your native language.

That being so, we should face the question squarely: "Why do I work?" I can accept that work is man's lot, and that it marks his dignity. "The other animals," says Milton's Adam, "unactive range, / And of their doings God takes no account." Man is not a creator, says Tolkien, but a "sub-creator," working in harmony with the creation that is given to him, and using his imagination to fashion things of use and beauty, and even fictional other worlds, such as Tolkien's own Middle Earth. But where does it say that the dignity of work depends upon being paid for it? If that were the case, then a whore selling her wares on a seedy street corner would claim greater dignity than my grandmothers could, who stretched a poor income to clothe and feed and in innumerable unnamed ways to bless my parents and their fourteen siblings between them. That makes no sense.

Perhaps we hire ourselves out when we do not need the money because otherwise we would have to face the question of what our lives mean. In other words, the busyness provides a welcome noise that distracts us from our spiritual depletion. Josef Pieper, in *Leisure: The Basis of Culture*, says that the characteristic sin of our age is *acedia*, usually translated as "sloth": a refusal or an inability to derive joy from what should legitimately bring joy, a sluggishness of spirit—the "noonday devil," as the early monastic writers called it. He says that sloth is quite compatible with a culture of "total work," wherein we value only what is difficult and what we must conquer our aversions to do. Midge Decter, in the book I have mentioned above, says that modern women envied not the freedom of men but their bondage, for men had no choice but to work at mostly unpleasant jobs to support their families. The women, Decter says, also wanted to have no choice, because the freedom of the home was too heavy a responsibility for them. They thus fled from freedom into Egypt, where they could rest their consciences while they dragged sledges of paperwork up the sides of social pyramids.

So women wanted to be injected with the same bacteria that infected the men already, and we see the predictable and perverse results. The sex that longs for the more for social life now flees the neighborhood, because the neighborhood is empty—no one is around; the neighborhood is a mere geographical construct, a block on a real estate agent's algorithm for calculating housing prices. She goes to work not to be alone, but work does not really satisfy those deeply human longings for friendship, shared sorrows, the simple pleasure of watching one another's children play together. Work in an office is not life in a neighborhood. Meanwhile the neighborhood is starved of women and their talents, children spend their lives suffocating indoors, men and women no longer accept their roles as gifts mutually given one to the other, divorce is common and never bothering to marry in the first place is commoner still, churches are sold and converted into antique stores while the supposedly antique virtues are despised, and the tasks of ordinary social life are handed over to institutions and bureaucrats, where they are performed badly, if at all. Why?

SEVEN

WORK WHILE IT IS YET DAY:
Making Good Things Again

Man is made to obey. He will obey either God or the one whom Jesus calls "the father of lies," a liar and a murderer from the beginning. There is no third choice.

If that is so, and if man is also made to be free, created in the image and likeness of God, who made all things not by necessity but by the outpouring of his own generous being, then freedom and virtuous obedience are one, as servility and vicious obedience are one. The slave is not the one who obeys. The slave is the one who obeys a vicious master, which may well be the man's own lusts. The free man obeys God. The slave is animated by lust, ambition, covetousness, servile cowardice, and envy. The free man is motivated by charity. The slave grumbles while he works, badly. The free man is like a grown son working for the father he admires and loves, whom the father trusts, and who has taken his father's authority into his soul. "The Son does only what he sees the Father do," says Jesus.

My question in this chapter is not what *work* we do for a living, but what work we do for a *living*: how to work in the light of day, for the sake of life, rather than subjecting life to work, or defining yourself and your life in the terms of work. It is how not to be a slave, even if you seem to be your own slave-driver. It is how not to collude in the servility of others.

Too Wealthy for Beauty—or Too Hurried?

The last time I was in Grand Central Station, I gazed at the long barrel vault above, a vast and noble conception, and wondered why we cannot have public works of this sort now. There are a few plausible answers, as I see them. The first, the one I hear most often, is that we do not have the money for it.

Let us follow this answer down the rabbit hole. We cannot afford beauty. That is a strange answer, because by any objective standard we are the wealthiest people in the history of the world. When I was a year old, my parents rented a tiny four-room house, two bedrooms upstairs, a kitchen and a parlor downstairs. The house had a "shower" in the coal cellar next to the boiler: it was a nozzle connected to a water pipe, with a drain built into the floor below. There were no walls around it. For a while we did not have a bathtub either. My mother took a few pictures of me taking a bath, at two years old, in an ashcan—a metal tub used otherwise for the sweeping of ash from the coal-burning furnace. I loved that house, where we lived till I was ten years old. By then I had a brother and two sisters, and it was not really comfortable to sleep two boys and two girls in a ten-by-twelve-foot room, even with bunks.

We went out to eat two or three times a year. Our vacations were visits to aunts and uncles and cousins (I have thirty-nine first cousins, not including their spouses and children). For the first ten years of my life, my favorite thing in the world was to go to a lake for a big family picnic, with my mother's brothers and sisters and their spouses and kids, and our grandfather and grandmother too. Our favorite lake was a big muddy pond that the owner of the land had dredged to provide a pretty fair area for swimming. He erected several big pavilions, for rent by the day. We ate grilled hot dogs and hamburgers—a growing boy like me would have three hamburgers at least, so hungry would I get from swimming and playing baseball. The aunts brought plenty of food. One of the uncles would go to the ice house (the last such in my hometown) with a couple of those ashcans, and that is how we kept our forty or fifty bottles of soda cold. Those sodas, from a local bottling plant, had names like A-Treat and Crystal Club and came in a variety of flavors, one or two of which are hard to find now: birch beer. The men brought beer, too, which was also brewed locally in Pennsylvania or upstate New York: Genesee, Gibbons, Schmidt's. We brought packs of cards, a horseshoe set, and wiffle bats and balls. We would get to the lake by eleven in the morning and not leave till after dark.

Then we moved into a new and roomier house, and my father had a swimming pool put in, and that was the end of our big family outings. I cannot find the old lake on any map. It was a small family business, one of many such in the area. Some of them had concession stands and arcades with games like skee-ball. Those are gone too. Call them a piece of Americana. We grew *too rich* to afford them. So instead of driving twenty miles to a lake with your big brood of kinfolk and making memories that remain with you for your whole life—my Aunt Irene trying to hit a wiffle ball with a swing as if she were trying to chop the head off a chicken, and complaining and laughing—you travel two thousand miles to a corporate amusement park like Disney World, spend thousands of dollars, stand in line for everything, buy overpriced kitsch for souvenirs, and allow yourselves to be bombarded by the politically correct. There are no aunts and uncles and cousins, and no peace. Junk is more expensive than the real thing.

We are wealthy enough to afford junk, and a lot of it, and too wealthy to afford what is beautiful and enduring. I am not an economist but an observer of human nature. Let us suppose I want to hire a carpenter to build, for a room that is going to be a library, a set of handsome floor-to-ceiling shelves. Of course I need the money to pay him. But I must also be willing to wait. And the carpenter himself? His craft does not require huge outlays of money at a school for the making of furniture. Its main requirements are patience, perseverance, love, pride in his workmanship, and time.

We have the wealth—that is really incontestable. But much of it is wasted upon a seething congeries of rent-seekers, more about whom shortly. And then much is spent badly, on what is ugly and stupid or both. In my parish church—and in all likelihood yours too—colossal sums were spent in the 1970s on the destruction of beautiful things. It costs a great deal of money to buy up old farms, cut them up into lots, and put up "mansions" on them—out of place, coldly distinct from one another and unrelated to the land they occupy, and strangely silent, for their owners are too rich to afford to have large families. It costs a great deal to devour most of the green space on your college campus building spiffy new exercise centers with weight machines and stationary bicycles all in a row, where fields used to be.

What we do not have is the *time*. That is not because we work longer hours than our grandparents did. We work poorer hours, and we spend hours getting to and from work, and since much of our work is frustrating, not fully human, servile, and indoors, we do not enjoy the natural rest of the body's recuperating from exertion. We have not the good sore arms but frayed nerves and a foul mood. "Time is money," we say, and that is why we claim to never have enough of it. But time is not money. Time is a twinkling of the eye in the endless sweep of eternity; it is that brief span wherein we dwell here on earth, among others like us and the wonders of the created world.

I am not asking people to use time more wisely. I am not asking them to *use* time at all. Saint Paul urged the people of Ephesus to *redeem the time*, to buy it back, as it were, because the days were evil. Time is not to be wasted, true. But what the Gospels see as wasting time and what we see are very different things. Recall the parable. A king was hosting a banquet to celebrate the wedding of his son, and he invited everyone round about to attend. But the invited guests were too busy with their affairs. One had just bought a field, another had just got a tip on some stock primed to rise any day, still another had a campaign stop to make.

This one was supposed to be present at the closing on a house in Palm Beach, that one had to drive her children to the day camp on her way to work at the old folks' home. All those people were using up plenty of time. That was why they were not prepared for the great moment when it came. The kingdom of God is at hand, says Jesus. He is near, he is at the gates, says Saint John. Now is the acceptable time, says the prophet.

Ars longa, vita brevis, goes the saying, its original Greek form attributed to Hippocrates, the ancient physician. The art is long to learn, and life is short. The paradox is that if you are talking about art, the more hurried you are, the less time you have. It is impossible to learn art in a rush. If you try to cram as much action into an interval time, like stuffing feed into a chicken in a cage, you may get *more* done, just as you will get a fatter chicken, but what you get done will be of poor quality, *or will be of a different kind altogether.* It will be a sort of industrial production, standardized, impersonal, sometimes slovenly, but not bearing the traces of a human hand or a human mind. It will be as if the human being had been absorbed into the machine, so that what had been a tool is now the master, and what had been the master is now a tool.

This is so whether we are talking about assembly-line construction of television sets, or the formulaic papers that high school and college students are assigned to churn out, or the endless shuffling of documents from office to office, or the pasting together of local newspapers from the five or six wire services and their own careless and predictable writers. Anthropologists evaluate the sophistication of a culture by the beauty of its artifacts, such as the decorated pottery of ancient Greece, items that you would find in an ordinary home. By that standard, how would we fare?

The Human Things

Here is an example of the fading of the human from the world of work, worship, and family life all at once. I use it for an illustration. The reader can no doubt think of fifty others.

All over Canada, churches that could not afford a tremendous pipe organ used reed organs instead, a musical instrument that was often found in private homes, too. I have quoted Walter Pater already as saying that all art aspires to the condition of music. Maybe we can then say, whimsically, that all artisanship aspires to the crafting of musical instruments. The reed organ would be a great case in point.

For it was a beautiful piece of furniture as much as it was an instrument. We own one made by the Dominion Organ and Piano Company, once located in Bowmanville, Ontario. It is about as tall as a sideboard, taller than an upright piano. It has circular stands projecting from each side, where you would set oil lamps. Its edges are fluted, its large sections pegged or dovetailed together. The pedals, covered with heavy embroidered cloth, have jagged edges at the top, hidden when the pedals are at rest, to keep mice from building nests inside. Each pedal, in fact, was cast with the words "Mouse Proof" and "Pat. Pending." A swivel stool with a cloth seat came with the organ too.

Of course hand-stenciled calligraphy identifies the instrument's maker and each of the dozen "stops," the knob-handled plugs that put various features of the organ in play. To "pull out all the stops" is to put *everything* in play—the bass coupler, the treble coupler, the tremolo, the "vox humana" (which was supposed to sound like a human voice, but sometimes sounds like a cat in distress), the principal, the diapason, and so forth, depending upon the particular instrument, because those organs are seldom exactly the same.

The reed organ can never go out of tune, just as a harmonica can never go out of tune, because the reed organ is a sort of gigantic harmonica. The action of the pedals swings an armature with a large leather flap like a sail, back and forth. That makes the air move around at random, rushing into the little chambers that open when you press the keys. A small metal reed inside each chamber, such as you have in a harmonica or a whistle, vibrates as the air flows over it, sounding a pitch determined by its length and thickness. Some organs have two or three ranks of chambers and reeds, connected to different stops, producing a different quality of sound depending upon which stop you pull out, or both sounds or all three at once. Some organs, emulating the great pipe organs, have two manuals, or ranks of keys, so that you can play one kind of "instrument" with your left hand while you play another kind with your right hand—trumpet on the left, say, and the softer flutes and violas on the right. The craftsmen came up with amiable ways of producing "special effects." For example, pulling out the tremolo stop frees up an axle to which is attached a kind of pinwheel; its spinning gives the sound a vibrato, like the voice of a soprano singing in *Carmen*.

It was fun to play, and when you weren't playing it, it would still be the most beautiful article of furniture in your parlor or a perfectly fitting item for your small church. If a key stopped playing, all you had to do was open the works in back, take out the "whistle" in question, and blow through it till you got the dust out. Everything else could be fixed by reattaching some piece of carpentry that had worked loose. A piano can be left untended for so long that the force of its tightening strings can eventually warp and crack the frame, and then the piano is firewood. That cannot happen to a reed organ.

Now then, you cannot give these organs away—no one wants them. No one can play them. No one knows the sacred or popular songs you would play on them. A few years ago I met a carpenter, a patient and skilled man, whose work includes the making of desks, hutches, and sideboards from old reed organs. He told me then that he was at work on his 176th such job. He turns great furniture of one sort into great furniture of another sort; but of course you cannot play "Nearer, My God, to Thee" on a secretary.

Maybe we draw near to the mark here if we simply confess that we do not have beautiful things because we do not want them enough. We do not have the time for them, meaning that we do not feel like taking the time that they require, not only to make but to enjoy. We do not truly love them. We do not sing "Nearer, My God, to Thee" because our desires are elsewhere. The freedom, the silence, the peace, the human dwelling in time—we flee from them, because they make us face our spiritual emptiness. We are stuck on the expressway from O'Hare Airport because the alternative, sitting still in our room, is too appalling. We lose the human things and replace them with inhuman things—anything at all, rather than nothing.

Shop, but Not at the Mall

What do we do about it, then?

When my nephews were in high school, they were required to take a semester of shop class, followed by a semester of home economics—cooking and sewing. The girls were required to do the same. As the reader must perceive, I am trying to champion all the things that human beings do with their hands, putting their minds and their hearts into the work, so that they become more human by it, not less; more like artists themselves, and less like the output of a Human Resource Machine. But the teachers at the school were not thinking in that way at all. The ordinary thing would be to require a year of one or the other, and let the boys and girls choose which one they wanted. In a year you might learn a good deal; but sanity had to yield to a political ideology.

To hell with the political ideology. If we step out of the way, we will see boys naturally gravitating towards the jigsaws and the routers, and girls toward the kitchen, and only our obnoxious fixation upon money-making and careers could ever persuade us that it is a worthy thing to make a chair but a base thing to make a cake—unless you are going to sell it.

But there's another problem. I have said that we should not be in a rush, because that is a great way to waste or kill time. Then it would seem that I would not want children to begin to learn a trade—to learn how to do good work with their hands—till they are finished with the ordinary twelve years of schooling. That is a dreadful mistake.

Young hands learn best. Suppose you try to become a baseball player at age twenty. It is impossible. There are hundreds of things you must learn only by years of doing. You will never get the feel of the bat or the ball; you will never know by instinct how the ground ball is going to skip; you will never understand what that particular sound of the bat hitting the ball means; you will not be able to gauge the flight of a fly ball in a breeze; you will not know whether you have enough time to get the batter out on a slow roller to third; your hands will be all thumbs. Can you begin to learn to make good furniture at age twenty? Yes, perhaps; you are not up against the constraints of age, as you would be if you tried to become a baseball player. But you would be at an enormous disadvantage.

What is it like to hammer a four-inch nail? A finish nail? What is the best way to tap the hammer on a nail-set? How do you "toe" a nail? What are the various kinds of clamps good for? How much can you bend a slightly crooked eight-foot-long two-by-four pine stud so as to nail it into place securely? What is the difference between a stud that is cut an eighth of an inch longer than the space where it is to go and one cut a sixteenth of an inch longer? What is the difference between pine and maple? Between maple and oak? How do you "rip" a board lengthwise, without shredding and splintering? How deep should you drill a hole for a wood screw? How wide should the hole be?

These are things you pick up without instruction from a book. Your hands learn them, and young hands learn best. You learn the "feel" of wood, or of the soldering iron, or of the trowel. You learn when the cement or the mortar is about right for the particular job—not too wet, not too dry, not lumpy. You learn about how much "mud" to put on your trowel to cover that hole. That is why, in the days before the government absorption of every human thing into itself, boys began to learn a trade while they were very young, if they seemed to have a knack for it. You became an apprentice, and if you persevered and improved, you would eventually be taken into the tradesmen's guild as a master, provided that you executed a work worthy of a master: a *masterpiece*.

Part of our problem is that those twelve years of schooling are in large part an enormous waste of time, because very little of the true, the good, and the beautiful is learned there. School is the asylum where we send children whom we do not know what to do with otherwise. They learn no grammar there, very little history, no geography, very little of their language's literary heritage. They get some math, but in a protracted and mind-dulling way, and some science, but very little of the world that is near their hands and eyes. Boys especially are bored to tears by it all, and then the remedy comes in the form of drugs, because they cannot pay attention to what is not worth attending to in the first place.

There is no conflict between being trained up in an art and acquiring a strong knowledge of the humanities: witness Michelangelo, who was also a great Italian poet. You can't always be at the work bench; sometimes you will want to read a good book, or sing good songs, or play wholesome games outdoors. School as it is now constituted wastes even more than time: it wastes *life itself.* It drags out its days and years in weariness, conformity to the political insanity of the day, writing by formula and not by art, and reading mostly junk, the educational equivalent of styrofoam, soft pornography, and mass-produced French fries.

So let us think again about what it means really to do good work—work that is good for man—and let us see about beginning when children are young and eager to learn it. We might not have the system of apprenticeships that people in times past took for granted, whereby a boy would learn a trade in exchange for his room and board. But we can—certainly homeschoolers can—revive something of that old cultural institution by way of an informal exchange of labor and perhaps some money for instruction—sweeping the shop, mowing the lawn, weeding the garden, stacking the wood, whatever would free the master's hands for his real work, in exchange for being nearby, watching, listening, and being given the more elementary tasks to perform. It was done before, and it worked splendidly. It can be done again.

No Work to Be Done?

Many years ago a Christian man who did volunteer work in the state penitentiary in Rhode Island told me that the prisoners were no longer given the opportunity to be instructed in a trade. Instead they were encouraged to take college preparatory classes. I thought that the policy was insane, and asked him about how many of the prisoners eventually went on to college. "About 5 percent," he said. "But the unions control the state legislature, and they pressured them to make this change in policy, because the local carpenters and electricians do not want any additional competition."

The fear of competition—of too many men entering the field and thereby driving down wages and the opportunity to work at all—is not idle, nor is it new. In fact, one of the reasons that the real earnings of working-class men in the United States have been stagnant for forty years is the mass exodus of women from the home and the neighborhood and into the labor force. That has also had the strange effect of driving up housing costs, and of segregating white-collar professionals from everybody else, as now a doctor will marry a lawyer or a bank executive will marry a professor. Then the double income goes to support one family with one or two children, rather than each separate income supporting a family with four or five children.

The medieval guilds were established for many reasons: to ensure a high quality of workmanship, to keep the prices charged for work from falling because of an overabundance of workers, to succor the widows and children of deceased members, to exercise political influence (especially in the Italian city republics, where you could attain nominal membership in a guild through family connections), and to bring the members together for worship and celebration. Our trade unions are a pale shadow of the full human reality of the old guilds, but it is still true that union members look askance at the training of new workers. I have read in a copy of *The Century* magazine from 1885 that union locals would take pride in going ten years without having instructed a single young man in the trade.

Yet there is an enormous amount of good work that could be done and plenty of money to purchase it. Again, we are the wealthiest people in the history of the world, and that means that we need not live with garbage. Let me give examples.

Ride a train on a sunny day from New York to Philadelphia. That is a little over a hundred miles, but along the rails you will see miles and miles of dilapidation and defacement—culverts scrawled with gangland graffiti and obscenities, the undersides of bridges heaped up with garbage, old fences rotting and falling apart, abandoned mills, disused stations, remains of telephone lines—all looking like something left over after wartime, except that in our case the war has been waged culturally, the damage done to family life and to the men who in other times might have kept such places from reverting to rot and filth.

Go to a section of a Rust Belt town where elderly people live in their old homesteads. Many of them can't afford much, but many others do actually have the funds to pay someone for the necessary carpentry to repair and restore their homes. The problem is rather that it is nearly impossible to find someone skilled enough to do the work. Near our house there is a handsome bridge, about a hundred years old, made of wooden planks and steel posts painted green, to match the verdigris patina on the copper plaque announcing the date of its completion. The bridge was compromised by a flood seven years ago and has been closed to traffic since. Eventually, I suppose, it will be condemned, taken down, and replaced by the usual ugly thing. It too could probably be repaired and restored, but it is hard to find someone who would know how.

So it is in many other regards. In the parlor of your house a handsome molding joins the wall to the ceiling. It is made not of wood but of plaster. You had some water damage last year and now that molding has crumbled in one corner. The easy thing to do would be to yank out the whole thing and replace it with wood. The hard thing to do would be to repair the corner. You would like to repair it, but who can do that? Even work that does not involve a special art, like a small plumbing job, is hard to get done, because you have to find a plumber with the time for it. My elderly father-in-law has a leaky heart valve, which he will get replaced right away. If it had been a leaky valve behind the wall of his shower, he'd be lucky to get it fixed in the next six months. A lesser problem would not be worth trying to call a plumber at all—so the work would remain undone.

It is simply not true that there is a fixed amount of work to be done "out there," so that the more carpenters you have, the less each one will earn. The availability of the carpenters encourages people to hire them for work that *might be done*. People who want things of beauty will pay for them, but first you have to show them that you can make things of beauty. And of course we have to raise people who are patient enough for beauty, which can never be had fast, on the cheap.

And then there is the government. I open an artery every year for government at all levels, most of it incompetent, destructive of ordinary social relations, tyrannical, redundant, parasitical, and perverse. If I complain, someone more pleased with the situation (because he butters his bread by it) will say, "But without government what would become of your schools and your roads?" As if that were an answer. The schools could all meet Mr. Wrecking Ball tomorrow, and we would be none the less literate for it. We might even be wiser, if we read good books. Home-schoolers, who teach their children at a tiny fraction of the cost of institutional incompetence, have demonstrated that result to anyone with eyes to see. But the roads?

I know of no conservative who has a quarrel with building roads. So after the government has taken that half penny from my dollar of taxes, what on earth does it do with all the rest that is worth the cost?

But let us look at the roads anyway. I am driving down the Merritt Parkway in Connecticut, and I pass below one bridge after another, fashioned in art deco style, built by men hired under the Works Progress Administration, one of President Roosevelt's attempts to put men to work during the Great Depression. They are beautiful bridges, and no one is exactly like another. It is a fine and human thing to behold, and many a man could say to his grandchildren, "I put this stone in place."

I understand that many economists now say that Roosevelt's policies actually ended up prolonging the Depression. I have no quarrel with them. But I do wish to observe an anomaly. We spend far more money on social welfare, in real dollars and as a percentage of federal outlays, than Roosevelt did, and what do we have to show for it? Forty percent of children born out of wedlock, whole generations of broken and never-quite-formed families, men checking out of productive work, and immense bloodsucking bureaucracies that perpetuate the pathologies they are supposed to cure. Given that we are going to spend the money, why must we spend it so irrationally and destructively?

Instead of social workers, administrators, deans, secretaries, and other handlers of paper and answerers of telephones, why do we not have a veritable army of skilled craftsmen to make our roads, bridges, sidewalks, plazas, and public buildings beautiful? Oh, there are not enough of them right now for the job, but again there might be, and there would be an endless supply of things to take care of. I suspect that there are several reasons why we will not soon see in every town such public works as the Merritt Parkway boasts. None of the reasons does us credit. One is that the training and hiring of craftsmen would shift funds away from women indoors and towards men outdoors, and that will be viewed as harming the women—even though the same men might then be able to marry and support a wife and their children. A second reason is that the policy would tend to strengthen rather than weaken the family, and the Metastate subsists upon family breakdown. A third reason is that we would have to revisit the strange idea that every child has to be in the Great Holding Tank until age eighteen. A fourth reason is that we just do not care enough for beauty to bother with it. We like to see the old works when we come upon them, but we are too impatient to make any new ones ourselves. We are prefabricated people.

Again we see that a variety of pathologies are really one and the same: the denial of the human person, male and female, made in the beginning in the image and likeness of God. Because we are not allowed to acknowledge the differences between men and women, we cannot enact policies that will benefit each sex but in different ways; because we deny the Sabbath, we end up both idle and harried at once, doing bad work, work that is bad for us, and a lot of it; because we forget God, we forget all of the transcendentals and end up dabbling in mud; because we confuse freedom with autonomy, we end up slaves to the Great Promoter of Liberty below, that liar; because we lie, our language itself grows rotten, and we can no longer give anything its right name, nor do we even know ourselves.

Rent-Seekers: The Undetected Extortionists

I will end this chapter with a reflection on a kind of bad work that is common in our time.

In the fifth book of Edmund Spenser's epic allegory, *The Faerie Queene*, the knight of justice, Artegall, comes upon a narrow bridge erected over a swift and dangerous river. Everyone who wants to cross the bridge—perhaps to sell his wares or his produce on the other side—has to pay a "passage penny" to the slave whose job it is to squeeze it out of him. The bridge is a necessity, but the land around it is owned by a wealthy man named Pollente. The name derives from Latin *pollens*, "powerful," but is also a pun on the English "poll," meaning head. A poll tax is a tax on your head, and a political poll is a counting of heads, even when they are blockheads. Each head is subject to the extortion. Pollente also has a daughter with golden hands and silver feet. She dwells in the castle above and is named Munera, for the bribes she takes.

Latter-day Pollentes and Muneras are still working in tandem, bribing the rich and "polling and pilling" the poor. They pay government officials so that they have sole control over whatever "bridge" their less fortunate or less favored fellow citizens need to cross to make a living. This arrangement provides them with plenty of wealth, for which they themselves do absolutely nothing. They are what we call rent-seekers: everything has to go through them, or it does not go at all.

If you try to cross the bridge on your own, Pollente comes after you with horse and spear, and he is used to fighting there, while you are not. Artegall meets him on the bridge anyway and eventually defeats him, lopping his head off after they and their horses plunge into the river below. Then, in disguise as Pollente, he enters the castle and deals with the daughter, Munera, to whom he shows absolutely no mercy. Artegall's iron man, Talus—representing that foundational principle of justice we know as the *lex talionis,* the law of retribution or retaliation—drags her by the hair to a window as she weeps and pleads and hurls her to her death below. Spenser believes that that is a fit end for those who use their power to oppress the poor.

So now we should ask, what institutions are "Pollente's bridge" today? Who are those whose work is parasitical upon the work of others, contributing nothing of their own? Or, who are the turnpike keepers, who compel people to go *through* them, rather than around them?

Obviously, Pollente is going to be a kind of middleman, but not all middlemen are going to be Pollentes. Wholesale merchants, foremen, architects, officers communicating between the government and the master builder, keepers of records, truckers, accountants, bankers—all are necessary in any complex economy or for any complex work for the public welfare. But when the middlemen outnumber the men who perform the fundamental work, or when the middlemen arrange things so that the ordinary citizen has to pass through one unnecessary strait after another, or when the middlemen merely use a happenstance advantage in order to batten on other people's work, then we have Pollentes by the millions.

To illustrate. My father had a high school education, when that meant a high school education and not something other or something less, and then he spent two years in the Army. When his two years were up, he came home and began to work in a foundry, but that didn't work out, since the foundry was far away and he and my mother wanted to get married and live near to their parents and brothers and sisters. "Home," it used to be called. So he got a job selling life insurance and disability insurance, on strict commission, no salary. He sold a policy on his first day and then did not sell another for one solid month. He was going to quit, but my mother told him not to worry about it, because she was confident in him, and they would get by. He stuck with it and soon became one of the company's top salesmen in the Northeast.

It has often occurred to me that what happened to him is unthinkable now. Insurance companies do not hire high school graduates. They cannot afford to take the chance. A high school diploma does not imply that you can do the math necessary for explaining insurance to your customers, and it offers no assurance that you will actually perform the work for which you are hired. They are also afraid of being sued for some form of discrimination, so they fall back upon a middleman to do the accrediting for them: they demand a college degree, which will very seldom have the slightest thing to do with the selling of insurance. *They* are not hurt by it, and the colleges of course are not hurt by it, but everyone else is. Squeeze through, young person, and pay handily while you go.

Then there are rent-seekers who go after the colleges in turn. College accrediting agencies, collectively, now own a bridge. These agencies used to be employed by the colleges to confirm that their account books were in order, that they actually did teach the courses that appeared on paper, and that the teachers were qualified to teach them. In other words, the accreditors were like investigators you hire to ensure yourself against accusations of fraud. But over the years the agencies have extended their reach. They now consider as their responsibility everything and anything that goes on in a college. They can do so, because they have pushed legislation allowing for it; the hand fits the glove. Therefore they grow immense, and the job takes longer and longer, and the colleges defer to them, afraid of a bad judgment. The accreditors now take it upon themselves to judge whether you live up to your stated mission—something they cannot possibly determine, not living at the school, nor necessarily understanding what the terms of the mission statement actually mean. That takes a lot of time and snuffs up a lot of money, and the very vagueness of the job makes it more expansive and expensive and threatening to the school, which then will hire additional deans and administrators to cover their bases.

Government is now a factory to produce rent-seekers. Each college has a "compliance officer," usually at least a lawyer with an office and a secretary, and sometimes other legal functionaries too, whose job is to make sure that the college complies with the thousands of regulations passed by government agencies without the direct knowledge of the people or their representatives. As these regulations grow more indefinite and more numerous, the job of complying with them grows also more arcane, requiring someone with special knowledge of the judicial and bureaucratic decisions the regulations have engendered. It is extraordinarily costly, the worst kind of make-work, and it has nothing to do with the life of the mind and the education of young people.

Rent-seekers can usually appeal in a roundabout way to the common good, but to the extent that they are removed from the people who actually do the fundamental work of the business or farm or school, they are very unlikely to be doing anything other than leeching onto the good provided by others. This truth applies to people in both public service and private enterprise, and especially to those who have a finger in both pies. When I was a boy my father gave me a diagnostic example of it. My grandfather worked for a few years as a deliveryman for a local creamery. He delivered bottles of cold milk (including a quart of cold chocolate milk for me) to people's doors. The milk was cold because the owner of the farm kept the bottles in a deep well fed by cold springs. Since his customers were local, none of the milk was ever bad, and everybody was satisfied.

Then came the men from the Food and Drug Administration to tell the farmer that he had to install large and expensive stainless steel tanks to hold the milk between milking and delivery. Now, the tanks would *not* do a better job than the wells had done, but the new regulation was what it was, and Mr. Cure would either comply or go out of business. Since he was getting along in years, he decided to fold up the works, and thus did a long-lived and much-esteemed local business meet its demise. My father said that the bigger suppliers of milk had publicly complained about the regulation but had actually colluded with the lawmakers to write the regulation in such a way as to compensate them for their additional expense by putting their smaller competitors out of business. "Do not believe that big business is not in favor of big government," said my father.

Interest groups, even with nonprofit status, act as rent-seekers when they have enough money and sufficient favor among unscrupulous judges to be able to threaten businesses, no matter how small, into doing as *they* please, lest they find themselves named in a costly suit. Family law is a vast spider's web of rent-seekers, who can eat up an entire estate and make somebody a wage-slave for many years, exactly insofar as the laws regarding custody of children and alimony are vague and subject to the caprice of the judges and the inventiveness and pertinacity of lawyers. If the law were to stipulate that the spouse admitting to adultery would under no circumstances receive custody of the children, there would be a lot less wrangling over divorce—and therefore a lot less work for family lawyers and judges, and a lot less profit for them. It is as Milton describes the hoary deep between Hell and the created universe, a vast vacuity of "embryon atoms" colliding with one another:

Chaos Umpire sits,
And by decision more embroils the fray
By which he reigns.

That right there gives you the *actual* constitution of the United States.

And we say, again, that we do not have the means to surround ourselves with things of beauty? We have the means. Each one of us has a pair of hands and a mind. Each one of us in his or her private capacity at least can reject bad work and repudiate the stupidities that keep us from raising craftsmen rather than bureaucrats. Time to do it.

EIGHT

PLAYING UPON THE WATERS:
Bringing Play Back to Life

Quite a while ago I was driving my daughter to her dancing lessons, when I saw something that made me gasp. We were passing by what used to be housing for Navy men stationed in Rhode Island but had been converted into apartments for the poor. In the large grassy area between the road and the buildings, about twenty boys, most of them in their teens, were playing a pickup game of football.

It suddenly occurred to me that I had not seen the like in a long time. I concluded that their poverty had something to do with it. Because they were poor, they were not spending their time in costly after-school programs, and because they lived cheek by jowl, there were enough of them to get up a good game, and because of the lie of the land, there was a big field for them to play football in, and because the old barracks were set at some distance from the center of town, there was nobody to complain that it wasn't "safe" and put a stop to it. In rich neighborhoods, you never see children outdoors without surveillance, and without coordination and co-option by the parents, who always have a weather eye out for what the children might eventually "do" with the sport they are learning to play. In other words, play is an extension of the soul-deadening thing called school and is preparatory to the soul-deadening thing called college and a career. In poor neighborhoods you still sometimes see children playing. I pass by a large middle school on my way to work, and early in the morning I will see a couple of platoons of boys playing touch football on a blacktopped area that used to be an outdoor basketball court. The boys are almost all black or Hispanic; it is another poor neighborhood, but they appear to be having a great deal of fun.

It is true that for some sports you really do need to have your father around to give you basic pointers in its hundred quirks and bounces. Baseball, for example: how to hold a bat, how to judge a pop fly, how to run the bases, how to slide, how to throw a curveball, and so on. That is why black Americans have been fading from the game in the last thirty years, their places being taken by boys from Latin America (Mexico, the Dominican Republic, Nicaragua, Cuba, Venezuela) and now from the Pacific rim (Japan, Taiwan, Korea). But for the most part, sports were passed along by boys to other boys, without the meddlesome adults to organize all the delight out of them. And then there were the games that never rose to the level of sports or were what you played when you did not have enough bodies for the real game: pepper, hit the bat, pickle, horse, one on one, and the immemorial games of childhood, such as hide and seek, kick the can, cops and robbers, and king of the hill.

These games constituted a childhood culture that was in part independent of the adult world and gave children a chance to be the lords and ladies of their own "society," with its habits, its laws, its entertainment, its rivalries, and its language. It is a deeply human thing. You could find it among Eskimos as well as among the natives along the Congo. You could find it among peasants as well as among the sons of rich men sent off to boarding school. You could find it among girls as well as boys, though they would not always play the same games. Saint Augustine played ball with the other boys in the streets of Thagaste, in North Africa, and in *Confessions* he says that he should have been doing his studies instead; I rather doubt that. We are the odd ones out. We are the people whose neighborhoods do not ring with the voices of children at play. A student of mine, an Eagle Scout, once told me that he had to teach the boys in his troop *how* to organize a game. They enjoyed it when he did that for them, but they could not do it themselves. In its way it was like never having learned to read; except that cultures that are oral and not literate can be vibrant. Perhaps it was like having been confined to a cubicle for the first ten years of their lives, so that they never really learned how to run or how to walk with strong strides. Such youths are cripples, not by nature, but by un-nature: crippled by neglect.

The Workout

I am looking at a painting by the great American impressionist Winslow Homer. It is called *Boys in a Pasture* (1874). Two boys, ten or eleven years old by the look of it, are sitting in a broad field under an open sky. One of the boys sits cross-legged, leaning forward a little, his arms wrapped around one knee. The other boy is lying back, propped up on one elbow. They are right next to each other, quite at their ease, looking at something in the distance that we cannot see. It is probably late spring, since the boys are wearing long sleeves, but it is warm enough for them to be wearing broad brimmed hats, one of cloth and one of straw, with the end tipped up. The boy with the arms around his knee has the broad wrists you get from farm work. Both of the kids have big, bony feet—for they are barefoot, of course. "The soil," laments the poet Gerard Manley Hopkins, "is bare now, nor can foot feel, being shod." Not so long ago, boys and girls went about in that direct contact with grass, flowers, dust, worms, and mud, with who knows how many salutary oils and earthy compounds to make the young body at home in the world, rather than to have its immune system react against a thousand natural things as if they were alien invaders from another planet. Bare feet, as you might surmise if you think about it for a moment, are also much better than shoes if you are going to climb rocks and trees. Toes grab. Shoes slip.

Here someone may object that Homer's painting is "not realistic," but that is precisely what it is. It depicts a scene that needs no introduction. Everyone in Homer's day would have known immediately what it was like to be those boys, even if he did not live in the grassy plains. Again we are the odd ones out. Someone else may object that life is "more complex" now, and that the days of such simple pleasures are past. More complex—really? Undoubtedly those boys did a great deal of work on the farm: important chores every day, tending animals; working with machines like harrows and plows; working with spade, hoe, mattock, ax, saw; working alongside older boys and men; different kinds of work depending upon the season and the weather; work that partakes of play, bringing food to the table by hunting, fowling, and fishing. And what exactly is so "complex" about being bused to an enormous school 180 days of the year, learning little, and coming home to watch television or play brain-rotting games on a computer? The very resting of those boys in the field is predicated upon good hard necessary work, work that would be making men out of them without anybody's having to think of it as a special project.

I am looking at another painting by Homer called *A Basket of Clams* (1873). The scene is a beach, with old weathered houses in the background and a dory that looks a bit worse for wear. It is a bright day, and the short shadows suggest that it is around noon. Two boys lug a large basket between them. The beach is littered with the usual things: shells, driftwood, a dead fish. One of the boys looks off to the side, clearly with an eye out for a promising spot to dig. They are barefoot. Now then— what exactly makes this scene impossible now? Or as rare as a pearl in an oyster? Is it that the ocean has dried up? Are there no more clams? People do not eat clams anymore? Clams are so cheap that they are not worth the finding?

A third painting by Homer, the well-known *Snap the Whip* (1872). For those born after the Great Severance—the severance of a generation of children from all the generations of children that came before—snap the whip is less a game than a rough-and-tumble spree of high spirits. A lot of kids line up hand in hand to make the whip, and then they run around and try by main strength and momentum to "snap" or "crack" the end of the whip, causing the last couple of kids to fly loose and tumble. That's what has happened in the painting: seven boys in the foreground have snapped the whip, and two boys on the end have tumbled free. It's a fall day, with tree-covered mountains nearby, along with the requisite red wooden schoolhouse. Two young women, the teachers, stand far in the background, looking on at a distance. The boys are barefoot, and most of them are wearing suspenders, because they will have work to do when school is out.

The painting would not make much sense now, for the most obvious reason—you need the nine boys, and they aren't generally to be found.

It is hard to get people to see things that are *missing,* but I would like to try here, to illustrate something strange that has happened to us. In all of Homer's paintings of childhood, you do not find adults organizing things: no camp instructors, no coaches, no lifeguards, no social workers, no police. That doesn't mean that Homer was a sentimentalist who thought that all children were perfectly innocent. He was painting shortly after the Civil War, and you could easily find scenes of destruction from Gettysburg in the north to Charleston in the southeast and Vicksburg southwest on the Mississippi. In yet another painting, *The Watermelon Boys* (1876), he has three young scapegraces in a field outside of a farm. There's a wooden palisade in the background, but one of the slats is broken and tilted, providing a nice hole for boys to squeeze through. Evidently the three boys—two black, one white—have done just that, and have hauled away an enormous watermelon, out of which they have cut big wedges, one for each. One of the boys, though, has stopped eating and is looking warily over his shoulder back towards the farm. Perhaps he hears some commotion from that quarter. He looks like he has a guilty conscience. The other two boys are so immersed in the delight of the watermelon, they don't hear a thing.

No strictures, no metal detectors, no watermelon checkpoints. And something else. *No equipment for the exercise of the body.* Plenty of equipment, sure—boats, oars, baskets, hooks, and suchlike, but that is equipment for the performance of some task. It was the blessed time before there was ever an exercise bicycle in the world. When the bicycle was invented, people used it to go places, even if it was to go someplace for the sheer pleasure of it. The idea of pedaling a bicycle that was riveted to the floor—that went nowhere—would have struck people as slightly mad, or sinister.

People had not turned what should be play into a form of work, and work that actually accomplishes nothing: it is work for work's sake, the "workout." Compare the things. Suppose you and your friend take your bicycles and ride down a country road. You stop at a spring for cold water. You are sometimes rocketing downhill, sometimes standing for leverage as your legs slowly pump the pedals and you zigzag uphill. Sometimes you may have to get off and walk the bike up. Sometimes you lay the bikes down and check out something along the road: a cherry tree, maybe. You are not exercising for the sake of it; you have not turned play into a grind; you have not isolated yourself with headphones; you are not monitoring your heart rate as if you were a machine and you were conducting tests upon it; you are not strangely divided from your body, as if it were a thing that had to be whipped into shape, and not you, your person.

We may think of it this way. How many hours do young people in college spend churning the pedals on bicycles that climb no hills or roll along no old roads, or pulling the oars on rowing machines that travel along no river, or heaving up heavy things and putting them down again, without a single stone being laid upon a stone? Now ask how many hours they spend dancing the Virginia reel or the waltz. Don't ask which *really* causes the healthy heart to race.

Human Materiel

Americans have a strange relationship with sport. It is a new thing in the world. It is sport that is governed not by the spirit of play, which is also the spirit of mirth and celebration, but by the spirit of work.

The demon Screwtape chastises his nephew Wormwood for being so foolish as to allow his charge, the young man to whose damnation

Wormwood is assigned, to take a pleasant walk to an old mill, through country he really enjoys, just for the pleasure of it. Wormwood has to be reminded that the Enemy (God) is a hedonist at heart, and that although the devils may use pleasures to tempt the little vermin, when they do so they are, so to speak, fighting upon the Enemy's territory. The devils have set about their laboratories for ages upon ages and have yet to create one true pleasure.

In *Homo Ludens* Johan Huizinga, the rare social historian with a firm grasp of the human things, relates the spirit of play with a certain freedom, even a reckless freedom. You do not play in order to amass counters in an economic struggle for dominance. Mirth, not grim seriousness, is the "rule," if that is even a proper word to describe the carnival atmosphere that allows for a merry misrule, a sacred space set apart from the workaday world. Huizinga's most startling example of such play comes from the Tlingit Indians of the Pacific Northwest. A rich man among the Tlingits will host a tremendous banquet, the "potlatch," for some special occasion, for example to commemorate the death of the chief of his clan. There he and his guests will consume a staggering portion of his goods, devouring them, giving them away, even putting them to the flames! And then in the following year one of his rivals will try to outdo him in conspicuous generosity or devil-take-the-hindmost liberty.

Play is not for the sake of work, just as, to return to Josef Pieper's wise and wonderful *Leisure: The Basis of Culture* the Sabbath is not for the sake of the other days of the week. The truly human and divine thing is to see the other days of the week in the light of the Sabbath, and not the Sabbath as a day for replenishing the human materiel so that it can work more efficiently on Monday. The Sabbath is the Lord's Day, not the slave driver's day. You cannot be grimly determined to love someone: it is a contradiction in terms. You cannot sweat at being merry, though being merry may well make you sweat—the good wholesome sweat of legs dancing and countenances flushed with glee. To ask, "What advantage do you gain from a square dance?" is to pose a question that admits of no other answer than a look of incomprehension.

You might as well ask what gazing at the stars has to do with stocks and bonds.

And yet what have we done with sport? We have transmuted it into work for children, first for boys and now for girls, as ambition and avarice invade every small corner of what used to be a free human life.

We know this is true. There is no gainsaying it. Parents boast that their children are in soccer, football (for boys), volleyball, swimming, and dance (for girls). In Canada it's hockey that rules, and parents will spend thousands of dollars a year per child for hockey equipment, instruction, camps, travel, and ice time, much of that travel and that ice time on Sunday, because the slight hope that a boy will become a professional hockey player means more to them than the hope that is in the name of the Lord, who made heaven and earth. "Why spend your money for what is not bread?" asks the prophet. And it is not bread. It eventually chews like grit between the teeth, like ashes. If someone should reply, "We are hoping that Joey," or Joanna, "will win an athletic scholarship to Land Grant State University," that is so much the worse, because now education itself submits to the demands of work for work's sake. Think of the tangle of contradictions. You subject your child to an athletic regimen for ten or twelve years so that he or she will be able to continue the regimen in college, where he (or she!) will be too exhausted to enjoy a good book at leisure or to engage in a free and relaxed conversation about important ideas.

Let us retreat a moment and ask what the difference is between two things: a group of boys playing baseball in someone's back yard and a Little League game. I do not wish to cast aspersions on the Little League, which does a lot of good work and which can partake of plenty of the spirit of play, if it is not turned into something grim and fearful. I have many fond memories of those games—the well clipped fields, the signs on the fence advertising local businesses, the older kids helping out as coaches or scorekeepers, the colorful uniforms, the concession stand for hot dogs and soda, the mothers sunning themselves on the bleachers and chatting—and when I was a teenager I enjoyed earning a few dollars as the umpire. Most of the kids were decent sorts, and only once did I have to threaten to call a forfeit because of an obnoxious fan, probably drunk, upsetting the game.

And yet—it is an "official" thing, involving regular practices, scheduled games, adult instruction and supervision, record keeping, monetary expense, and ordered competition. None of those are bad things. Ordered competition is in itself a very good thing, one of the foundational stones of Western civilization: the Greeks invented the free self-governing city-state, the *polis*, in the context of the *gymnasia* and of the special games that all of the Greek men would celebrate together at Olympia in honor of Zeus or at Delphos in honor of Apollo. But ordered competition, arranged and controlled by adults, should not be *the only thing*.

When children come together to play, we see in miniature the very art of culture itself. It is by no means a simple and obvious thing. Let us say you have a bat, a ball, a vacant lot at the back end of a building, a fence about a hundred and fifty feet away, a large maple tree to one side, and eleven boys. Two of them are small, only seven years old. One of them is fifteen, three years older than the next oldest. It's a very warm day in summer, and there are no objects around to serve for bases. You want to play ball. What do you do?

You see that there are no adults to do the thinking for you. You have to adapt the game to the circumstances. This adaptation is a deeply human thing. You want it to be a "good game," a game in which the sides will be fairly even, because otherwise there is not much fun in it. You cannot have the oldest boy give a lopsided advantage to one of the teams. Since you have an odd number of players anyway, you decide that he will pitch for both sides—which of course he is glad to do, since he will be involved in every play. The two littlest boys also have to be on separate teams. That said, you "choose up sides," with the leader of one team picking a player, followed by the leader of the other team. If that still results in an imbalance, you adjust sides accordingly, exchanging one player for another. The boys understand that there is nothing personal here; that means that they put their feelings aside for the sake of the game, for the sake of the sheer fun of it.

The tree is in the way, so you have to invent a ground rule to deal with it. Which ground rule? It depends upon the character of the tree, its placement, and whether you are all right-handed batters. You may decide that anything that hits the tree in fair territory is a live ball, and let things fall as they may. You may decide that the whole area around the tree is off limits: any ball that hits a branch of the tree is out. You may decide that if a *right-handed batter* hits the tree, he is out, but for a left-handed batter it will be a live ball.

You don't have anything for bases, so four of you volunteer your shirts. The littlest boys have trouble swinging the heavy bat, so you decide that the pitcher will toss the ball to them underhand. The ball is made of rubber, so you talk about whether you should allow "throwing at the runner" for making an out. You decide that if a ball rolls under the fence in the outfield, it will be a ground rule double. Anything that goes over the fence on the fly is a home run. There will be no taking leads off the base.

And so on. You have to decide on the batting order, and remember to keep to it. You have to keep track of the strikes and the outs and the score.

You have to be able to resolve the inevitable disputed plays. If the pitcher is common to both teams, he can also serve as the umpire. If not, then you go through a rather intricate series of claims and counter-claims, appeals to honest observers and to evidence, and if nothing settles it, you decide to do the play over again, as if nothing at all had happened; and the boys set their aggressiveness and rivalry and selfishness aside and submit to this cardinal rule, so that the play might continue.

And there is much more. How do the boys come together in the first place? How do they know when to end the game? What are they doing when they are waiting for their turn at bat, or just standing in the field? What do they do once they are soaked with sweat and the game is over? All kinds of human things. They talk. They rest. They tell jokes. They decide in a small platoon to go to the store for drinks. On long summer days the only clock was the slow sun moving through the sky. They play cards. If there's a river somewhere or a swimming hole, they go there.

Human beings are not materiel. How have we forgotten this?

A Tangle of Errors

A commercial is now airing in Canada, the nanny state of the north, urging parents to allow their children to play freely, without always being under the direction of adults. The Canadians are quite right about that, as are the Americans who urge children, in a public service announcement, to "play sixty," that is, to play at least sixty minutes a day, for their health. We might as well urge them to eat and drink, to walk, to look about them, to talk to their brothers and sisters, and to play with the family dog. The astonishing thing is that these things would ever have to become the object of national exhortation.

What is left unsaid, though, is that we have dismantled an entire cultural structure that allowed for a true childhood. We have fallen into a tangle of errors, one error looped and knotted around another. When you try to free yourself from one, you find that you cannot do it without resolving another one, a more fundamental error. Chesterton illustrates such a tangle in *What's Wrong with the World*, denouncing British public health officials who wanted to contain the spread of lice by cropping the hair of "all little girls whose parents were poor," children who were "forced . . . to crowd together in close rooms under a wildly inefficient system of public instruction." The doctors "propose to abolish the hair. It never seems to have occurred to them to abolish the lice." The "red hair of one she-urchin in the gutter," writes Chesterton, ought to "set fire to all modern civilization."

> Because a girl should have long hair, she should have clean hair;
> because she should have clean hair, she should not have an
> unclean home; because she should not have an unclean home,
> she should have a free and leisured mother; because she should

have a free mother, she should not have an usurious landlord; because there should not be an usurious landlord, there should be a redistribution of property; because there should be a redistribution of property, there shall be a revolution.

We might revise, so: Because children should be able to play freely outdoors and for hours on end, there should be neighborhoods for them to play in. Because there should be neighborhoods, there should be in those locales the natural though informal monitors of the neighborhood: elderly people on their porches, many mothers, and men and women at work in family businesses nearby. Because there should be such neighborhoods filled with people, our social policies should favor them and support them, and our cultural expectations likewise. Therefore we should not subordinate the family to work; the double-income family should not be the norm; we should reconsider all things that tend to remove father and then also mother far from the place where they live.

Or so: Because children should be able to play freely outdoors and for hours on end, the children themselves should be reasonably reliable, taking the moral law into their lives and desiring to be virtuous. Because children should be strengthening not only their arms and legs and backs but also their souls, they should have parents who observe the moral law, or at least wish to give the public appearance of observing it ("vice's tribute to virtue"). Therefore public policy and the customs that it corroborates should reward men and women who wait until they marry to have children and who stay together rather than divorce; fornication should be condemned as what it is, irresponsible and vice-ridden, a crime against children and the family.

Or so: Because children should be innocent in their play, their schools should not be seething beds of filthy habits; therefore they should be overseen by parents and not merely by "professionals"; therefore teachers who are models of immorality should be let go as a matter of course; therefore what children read should be wholesome rather than morbid, pornographic, or motivated by sexual politics.

You do not feel comfortable sending your child outdoors to play. Of course you don't. You have no neighborhood, only a geographical area. You have no local school. You do not know any of the mothers nearby. Old people live far away. Everyone is indoors or in a sports corral somewhere. Small businesses are gone. Responsible people are never to be seen, because they are at work, both mother and father. They live too wealthy a life to afford more than a couple of children, so that you never have a sufficient number of children just roaming about to get going a game of anything much. The older people do not play cards with one another. No one visits anyone. Hospitality—your home's openness to anyone who might show up at the door, any day, any hour—is a thing of the past.

Moloch, American Style

And why should we be surprised?

At the 2016 national convention of a major political party, the crowd cheered wildly when a woman stood before them and boasted that she had snuffed out the life of her child in the womb. Avarice, you have met Lust already. Now meet Murder.

The child kicks in the womb. He is stretching his legs. He is reacting with a flurry of motion to the strange things he hears in a muffled way coming to him from another world, a world that is only a few inches from him. When he is born, what does he do? He feeds. He looks with wonder upon colors, movements, things that are alive, things that make noise. He looks with wonder upon his mother, whom he knows, and upon his father, whom he comes to know immediately. He plays.

It is intellectually and spiritually incoherent to believe in the innocent play of children when you are willing to sacrifice them upon the altar of your ambition, your avarice, your lusts, or your convenience. You cannot suppress the reality of the child without amputating your humanity and searing the wound with bitumen and pitch.

The ancient Carthaginians used to make little babies "pass through the fire to Moloch," as the Scriptures say. Some historians used to accuse the Carthaginians' perennial enemies the Romans of fabricating the charges, but they can do so no more. We have uncovered a great necropolis near Carthage filled with bones, the little bones of babies. The Carthaginians were not an especially bloodthirsty people. They were businessmen; Chesterton imagines them as Victorian bankers in black frock coats and top hats. That is the point. The Carthaginians served up their children to Moloch because they believed that the fertility god was *economic* in the most exacting sense: if you want bountiful harvests, you had better give up some of the products of your own fertility. It was an exchange; it was what went on at the Wall Street of Carthage. If you were rich, you could buy the baby of a poor woman and claim the sacrifice as your own.

We do the same. We kill children for the sake of a richer paycheck, a nicer house, a nifty vacation to Cancun, a college degree, admission to the bar; or to avert having to stretch the paycheck, to sell the second car, to forgo the vacation, to drop out of college, or, as a feminist writer once put it, shuddering in disgust, to buy extra-large jars of mayonnaise at Costco. If we kill children for these things, we certainly will not scruple to put them in straitjackets, or to let them languish in the infested schools, or to sit them in front of a screen that is at best novocaine for the mind, at worst positively toxic.

"Unto us a child is born, unto us a son is given," said the prophet Isaiah. "Except ye become as little children," said Jesus, "you shall not enter into the kingdom of God." In his painting of the Last Judgment, Fra Angelico places a group of children, hand in hand with angels, in a flower garden, dancing. Have we forgotten what life is for?

NINE

IDIOTS NO MORE:
Recovering the Polis

The long-wandering Odysseus is seated as the guest of honor at the banquet table of Alcinous, the kindly king of the Phaeacians. He has finally revealed his name, at the special urging of the king, and now he has begun to tell the tale of what happened to him and his crewmen after they sailed from Troy.

We should notice first that Phaeacia is a *political* place, that is, a place where men gather together to determine upon courses of action for the common good; where people celebrate feasts in common; where things necessary and becoming for a good life are provided by farmers, sailors, merchants, shepherds, cultivators of the grape and the olive, potters, weavers, masons, and smiths; where customs of decent behavior for men and women are observed; where hospitality is extended to the stranger; where the gods are feared and praised. Far from being a despot, the king seems to govern rather by giving his opinion and suggesting it strongly to the elders, or by taking good counsel from others, including his wise consort, Queen Arete. One word from the queen, says the princess Nausicaa to Odysseus newly washed up on the beach, would suffice to win him what he needs to return home. And indeed it is to Arete that Odysseus appeals, as he sits as a supplicant near the hearth, and his measured and meek words gain her approval.

The Phaeacians are not saints. Homer makes no such claim for them. They are often contradictory or refractory, as all human beings are. Nausicaa does not want Odysseus to walk to the palace in her company, because she is afraid of the cat-calls from the men at work in the fields or the roads; they would tease her about her having found a strange man for her husband. That is Nausicaa's way of keeping herself free from rumors and putting the idea of marriage in Odysseus's mind—for she has eyed him up as a real man. When everyone is outdoors for the games—Odysseus has still not identified himself—one of the boys challenges him rather rudely, saying that he probably isn't very good at sports, knocking about the world as he has. He earns for his pains a rebuke from Odysseus, who tosses the discus (a big flat stone) a good deal farther than anyone else's mark. When Odysseus later wakes on the shore of Ithaca, where the Phaeacian sailors leave him, he believes at first that they have betrayed him and robbed him. Still, they are good people, and their *polis* is well governed. We are to compare Phaeacia with what we know is going on at the same time in Ithaca. One hundred and eight arrogant suitors for the hand of Penelope, the wife of Odysseus, are guzzling the absent king's wine and devouring his cattle and seducing some of his maids. They have turned his household into a place of shameless carousing and disorder. They have by now even conspired to kill Odysseus's son, Telemachus, who is on the verge of manhood and is now wise to their evil ways. Ithaca without Odysseus is a land of misrule.

So then, Odysseus is telling his tale to Alcinous and the guests, and he reaches the time when he and his ship put ashore at the island of the Cyclopes. Everyone remembers that a Cyclops is a hideous giant with one eye in the middle of his forehead, and that he is glad to devour human flesh. But the Cyclops is also one of many examples, in the *Odyssey*, of people who are sub-political, and *that* is the first thing we are meant to notice about the island. For Odysseus reckons up the place with the eye of a landsman and a leader. The Cyclopes have excellent bottom land for growing grain; the fields lie overrun with weeds. The Cyclopes have wild grapes growing everywhere; they do nothing with them. They have a harbor for ships; they do no sailing. They herd sheep, and that is all. They have no marketplace. They have no assemblies. Each Cyclops is the despot over his wife and offspring, and every family ignores its neighbors.

The Greeks had a name for someone who refused the opportunity to live a truly political life, that is, a life involved in local affairs that bear upon the common good. Such a person was all bound up in himself, his goods, his pleasures, his work. He was an *idiotes*, an idiot, and not because he was slow in the brain. He might be a quick-witted fellow and still be an idiot: still entirely focused upon himself. The Greeks had another name for someone who did not have the opportunity to live a truly political life. Such a person would not be speaking Greek, since if you were Greek you lived in a *polis*, from Halicarnassus on the coast of Ionia, to Corinth on the great isthmus, to the island *poleis* of Lesbos and Naxos and Melos and Delos and Rhodes, to Athens and Sparta on the Peloponnesus, to Epirus on the coast of the Adriatic, to Croton in southern Italy, to Syracuse in Sicily. Wherever the Greeks went, they established a *polis*. Other people spoke a language that sounded to them like bibble-babble: hence *barbaros*, babbler, barbarian. The barbarian is not someone who lets the blood from the pudding dribble down his mouth while he eats. The Persians had a great and efficient empire, and a high civilization, but they were *barbaroi* anyway, because they did not have the *polis*. They were ruled by an emperor from far away, and his professional armies, and his vast cadres of officials. They had no effective say in how they were ruled. Of course, barbarians might also be men who refused any rule at all, and so the suitors at Odysseus's home in Ithaca are *idiots* because they think only of themselves, and because the Ithacans have gone twenty years in Odysseus's absence without once gathering for an assembly; and they are *barbarians* because when Telemachus finally does call them to account before the Ithacan elders, they threaten him and his supporters with violence, effectively putting an end to the last traces of truly *political* life in Ithaca—until Odysseus returns unexpectedly.

The Word, but Not the Reality

I have engaged in this meditation upon the *Odyssey* for several reasons. First, it was the Greeks who gave us the very word, *polis*, from which is derived our word for action that has to do with the passage of laws: *political*. Second, it was the Greeks who invented the study of political structures: Aristotle famously says, in his *Politics*, that man is a *zoon politikon*, a political animal. Third, the Greeks bequeathed to us also the form of government we have or believe we have, in part: *democracy*. And yet—this is my most pressing reason—those same Greeks would not recognize what we have as political at all, but as a corruption of the political, transformed into the barbaric, and transformed in part by our cultivation of idiocy.

Return to the Cyclopes. Their land is rich but unemployed. Suppose that some imperial legate from far off Sousa were to oversee the growing of wheat and barley on the island of the Cyclopes. Suppose that the fields produce an excellent crop, which then the bureaucrats and middlemen trade for tin from the mines in Scythia. The Cyclopes live in the vicinity of all of this and occasionally go to the new Persian bazaars where items are sold that were acquired by trade. But the Cyclopes otherwise retain all of their old habits, with one minor exception. Every four years, the Persians elect a new emperor, and every citizen gets to cast a vote, one out of ten or twelve million.

Now there's a democracy? There's a genuinely political life? It is the life of barbarians, with the machinery of elections and the life of idiots, concern for the common good ceded to a governing class of bureaucrats.

Sometimes a *reductio ad absurdum* helps us clarify what is really going on. Let us suppose that Earth were a member of a Star Trek federation of a hundred planets flung across the Milky Way, each planet populated by ten billion rational beings, making a total of one trillion—one million million. Let us suppose that the federation is "democratic," meaning that each citizen casts a ballot for High Imperial Galactic Grandee. There are galactic pollsters, galactic news bureaus, galactic congressmen and senators, galactic executive agencies, galactic bureaucrats, galactic economists, and galactic businessmen skimming galactic profits off the top of galactic farms and mines and quarries and fisheries and so forth. Wouldn't that be wonderful? Just think of it. Your vote, one out of one million million, will help to decide galactic policies for the next four years. Will help, yes, certainly, just as a flea can influence the movement of a charging elephant. Or rather a tiny part of a flea—a flea-hair or a flea-pimple or something similarly infinitesimal and inconsequential, something that would hardly suffice to influence the flea, let alone the elephant.

Aristotle said that the ideal *polis* would necessarily be fairly small, small enough for you to know every other citizen by face or reputation or family name. Otherwise you are going to be ruled by people you do not know in any real sense, and by their ministers, from far away. Athens, with its forty thousand voting citizens, was about as large as a *polis* could reasonably grow without undergoing a change in kind: without becoming a very different sort of thing.

Or let us look at the matter from the small end of the telescope. Whatever is good about democracy rests upon a simple assumption. It is that ordinary people are capable of managing their own ordinary affairs, as individuals, as families, as members of a neighborhood or a parish, as local businesses, and as citizens of a village or town. If they are not permitted to do so, they have been reduced to what the Greeks called barbarism. If they are unwilling to do so, they have reduced themselves to what the Greeks called idiocy. Electoral machinery has nothing necessarily to do with it. A mother and a father working on a farm in Iowa in 1884 might worry about the price of silver set by the federal government, as it would have an effect on what profit they could make from their land, if they had borrowed against the value of the land to buy equipment, or if they had invested in additional acreage. They might worry also about what the railroads would charge them for freight, and whether the owners of the railroads had formed a cartel to keep the charges high. In good years they would not even worry about that. And then what?

What would James G. Blaine, the Republican candidate for president of the United States, or Grover Cleveland, the Democrat, have to say about how you ran your schools—whom you had to hire, what books you could use, what books you could not use, what you had to teach and when? It's true that the odious "Blaine amendments"—state laws based on a failed amendment to the U.S. Constitution authored in 1875 by then-Congressman Blaine—ensured that state moneys could not go towards the education of children in Catholic schools, supposedly because Catholic children would be obedient to another head of state, the all-dangerous pope of Rome, then living as a prisoner in the Vatican, the Papal States having been seized by Garibaldi and the Italian nationalists. Had Blaine been true to the spirit of democracy, he would have remembered that he was a congressman and not a county commissioner or school board member. But otherwise, Cleveland and Blaine would have nothing at all to say about education. Is it all right to mention Jesus in a commencement speech? Why would you even ask such a thing? Are you not a free people? What would they say about the price you were permitted to charge for a bushel of wheat? Nothing. What would they say about how you staffed your constabulary? Nothing. Curfews? Nothing. Whether your businesses should remain open on the Sabbath? Nothing.

What would these same candidates have had to say about whether the local Raccoon Lodge had to admit women? Nothing. Whether the Ladies' Beneficent Society had to admit men? Nothing. How you maintained your roads? Nothing. What you could or could not do with the swamp in back of your barn? Nothing. Whether you had to strap your children in when they rode on the back of the wagon? Nothing. Whether a man could use the women's privy? Nothing. Whether the manager of a hotel had to give rooms to unmarried couples? Nothing. How you could punish minor offenders like thieves and drunken brawlers? Nothing.

What is a town for now? What is left for ordinary people to decide, coming together in local assembly? Not much. Garbage pickup, perhaps. In the United States in 1920, there were twenty-one times as many school boards per thousand students as there are now. That means that twenty-one times as many people were involved in the running of schools. But even such school boards as remain hardly have much to discuss. Rules are handed down to them not only from the state capital, which is already something of an intrusion, but from Washington, and the members of the boards are usually also members of the teachers' unions, or relations of the teachers, or former teachers, crowding out the ordinary parents or talking them down.

My point is not simply that the farther away you are from the school—or the bridge or the bakery or the bandstand or the chambers of the justice of the peace—the likelier it is that your work will be expensive or otiose or impractical. It is not simply, to put it this way, that a neighborhood is *best organized by neighbors* and not by emissaries from Washington, the Kremlin, Brussels, or the United Nations. It is that when you take from people their authority, you rob them, as the Greeks saw, of something essential to their full humanity. Suppose the absurd could be demonstrated, that a government agency, a National Lunch Administration, would be more competent than you are to prepare meals for your children to take to school. They can't do it, but suppose they could. You would be forced to trade, for an extra 3 percent of the recommended daily intake of niacin and thiamine, the very gift of yourself that making the lunch constitutes. You would to that extent cease to be a mother or a father, becoming instead a ward or a client, or rather a somewhat unreliable thing-or-other in a machine, which the inventors and caretakers of the machine would someday be pleased to eliminate altogether.

It is not that everything has been politicized. Everything has been *stolen from the polis* and given over to Jabba the State—bloated, disgusting, corrupt, without conscience, accountable to no one, and voiding the resultants of his meals into the land and the drinking water and the air that everyone has to breathe.

We want our authority returned to us—or we intend to take it up again—because it is ours by right. We want not to be reduced to idiots and barbarians with a nominal and trivial vote. Our opponents here talk a great deal about *diversity,* which seems only to refer to the variously mottled patches of flesh over Jabba the State's tumid paunch. We want a diversity that strikes terror into their hearts: the natural diversity you get when the school board of East Springfield hires and fires and orders books with a different plan in mind from that of the school board of West Springfield; or when the Christian baker conducts business by his best lights, and the Jewish baker by his; or when men congregate to do something more conducive to the common weal than watching a ball game and getting drunk; or when women organize a father-daughter dance and do not thereby mean a mother-daughter dance or anything else besides what the words obviously denote; or when the citizens of North Springfield begin their meetings with a prayer; or anything else, Jabba, that is not your business, or yours, Jabba's creatures otherwise known as lawyers, college professors, social workers, and judges.

The Principle of Subsidiarity

Some of my readers will recognize that I am invoking what Roman Catholic writers on social issues call the principle of *subsidiarity.* The principle is easy to express, but the reasons why it is valid are subtler and more profound than most of its advocates seem to recognize. Simply put, the principle states that social concerns should be left to the smallest group that can reasonably deal with them, the group that is nearest to the concerns in question. If the family can deal with it, then it is not the problem of the neighborhood; if the neighborhood, then it is not the problem of the village; if the village, then it is not the problem of the county; if the county, then not the state; if the state, then not the nation. We do not want a national committee to send official Diaper Changers to every home with a little baby in it. Nor do we want a state committee to send official Book Orderers to every school with an English teacher in it.

People usually justify the principle on the grounds of practicality. They say that the farther you are from a human problem, the more likely it will be that your "solutions" are abstract and ineffective, because they miss the specifics; you will be prescribing the same social medicine for street boys in the Bronx as for runaway farm boys hitchhiking through Kansas, but the boys are not the same, and their virtues and vices are not the same. What works in rural Iowa will not work in urban Illinois. What works for men fleeing oppression in Cuba will not work for men fleeing the narcotics police in Mexico. Beginning the school day in a Tennessee village with a prayer will have the salutary effect of uniting the children and suggesting to them that there is something reverend about school, something set apart from the workaday world. Beginning the day that way in New Rochelle might have that same effect, but you would have to be careful to form the prayer so as not to put Christians and Jews on opposite sides of a fence. Ruling that *no school in the nation* may begin the day with a prayer, because *some school in the nation* might not do it well, is to reduce grown people to the status of children who cannot be trusted with the most ordinary things.

It is also to add layer upon layer of middlemen, like the false flesh that grows thick and covers the throat in diphtheria, suffocating the patient. Consider the case of school prayer. Once upon a time, when people were not treated as refractory children, the people who administered a school would decide how to begin the day, and that was that. When the Supreme Court Royal— turning the Constitution of the United States into a *carte blanche* for centralized domination over, or obliteration of, culture itself—took that authority away, that was not the end of the matter. People resented the expropriation, as anyone would have been able to foresee, and the result over more than fifty years has been endless litigation at all levels, to the great benefit of lawyers, with taxpayers suffering the expense.

So it is whenever the big and faraway attempts to manage the small and near. What sports teams should your college finance? That is eminently a local question. It has to do with what kinds of young people make up your student body, how big your school is, what sports will have the biggest draw from people in the vicinity, what your traditions have been, and what the mission of your school is. But the infamous Title IX of the Civil Rights Act, perversely interpreted by the Supreme Court

Royal to ensure that nobody will ever be certain what the law is and how it is to be applied, has resulted in immense monetary and human losses, as schools are compelled to offer athletic scholarships to women whose sports do not redound to the benefit of anybody other than the few women who play them, to eliminate men's sports in order to adjust the numbers aright, and to hire compliance officers who bring down big salaries for making sure that the schools somehow stay on the leeward side of the ever-changing weather of the law. Before Title IX, the most popular women's sports in the United States were tennis, gymnastics, and golf. More than forty years after Title IX, the most popular women's sports in the United States are still tennis, gymnastics, and golf, with an ambiguous nod towards basketball. This social change has been accomplished at the expense of many billions of dollars.

So regulation from above is awkward, ineffective, often counterproductive, and hugely expensive. Yet none of that is the real reason why we affirm the principle of subsidiarity. We must try to remember what it is to be a human being endowed with *reason*. Man, said Aristotle, cannot by himself live a life much higher than that of a brute. Without social groups, he has to live hand to mouth, eating what he can find or kill and sleeping in caves. We need one another, and our needs are more than material. They are social, intellectual, aesthetic, and spiritual. The distinction that people draw between man's nature and his nurture is factitious. It is entirely natural in man to form societies, and the kinds of societies he forms spring from his physical and intellectual nature. Therefore, if you rob man of his motives for forming social groups, or if you restrict the authority of those groups so that they have nothing important to do, or if you compel the groups to admit both men and women (when it is also natural in man to form some groups made up of members of one sex only), then you rob man of much of his humanity. You reduce him to a serf, even if he is a rich serf; though the serfs on a feudal manor probably had a richer social life than does modern, atomized, infantilized, institutionalized man under surveillance by his betters.

Eventually the social fibers atrophy. People cease to be able to run a school. Family ties linking the generations disintegrate. A sense of local identity fades. Parades (except, in large cities, those designed to celebrate what is vicious, puerile, perverse, and destructive of the family) are largely a thing of the past. The churches grow empty. Wednesday evening lectures on theology, community singing—what are they? Block parties are rare or unheard of. There is no "community chest." There is no Welcome Wagon. When I was a child, a local shoemaker would come out of his shop on every school day to help the school children cross our Main Street. It was an informal thing, and he was absolutely reliable. No more. The atomization sets in at all levels. Chess clubs, bridge clubs, local base-ball teams, reading groups, historical societies, drama clubs, fraternal organizations all begin to fade and disappear. No doubt there are other villains besides the all-mothering and all-smothering and all-devouring central government and its armies of bureaucrats and lawyers; the television, most obviously. All of the mass phenomena are implicated. But when a man is afflicted with diabetes, it is no excuse to give him cancer as well; or when he is undernourished already, it is no excuse to starve him.

What to Do?

Let your imagination run free.

The first thing to do is to persuade yourself that the central government's arrogation of power is illegitimate. The American Constitution was written to provide for a more effective governing body to unite the states—to form a "more perfect union." But it was also written to allay fears that the states would cease to exist as such, becoming instead what they are now, administrative provinces not only subordinate to the central government but also controlled by it for almost every conceivable purpose. For many decades after the Constitution was ratified, people used the plural verb when the "United States" was the subject of the sentence, reflecting the sense that a state was just that, a state, a self-governing society. Even the most aggressive centralizers among the Federalists, men such as Alexander Hamilton, entertained no vision of the vast administrative state that has combined with the judiciary and, in part, with the executive, to leave the people's representatives toothless and to leave their nearer political bodies boneless as well. Men who risked their lives and their sacred honor for the rights of Englishmen under the Common Law and for the principle that lawmakers ought to be directly accountable to the people for their actions can hardly have foreseen the mountains of regulations that have the force of law, without any lawmaker ever having voted for them, or even being able to tell what they are, and why.

The Constitution is not, as Charles Evans Hughes put it, whatever the judges say it is. It is the law of the land, and it belongs to each branch of the central government, to the states, and to individual citizens and the political and social bodies they form. The lawyers on the Court Royal have, we hope, the competence to determine what a law says, how a law applies to a particular case, and whether one law conflicts with another. They are possessed of no special wisdom regarding *what the law ought to be*; they are not social prophets; they know no more about human nature than does anyone of similar intelligence; they are not particularly well-versed in history, in the science of government, in industry, in the relations between the sexes, in international trade, in medicine, in schooling, in family life, or in anything else that has nothing directly to do with the law as such. *For that very reason* we have, or are supposed to have, citizen legislators, because any one person's stock of reason is going to be modest at best, and his stock of experience more modest still. Every time the Supreme Court Royal and its subordinate Courts Jester have exceeded the limits of their competence—every time they have refused to mind what business is rightly theirs—the results have been nugatory at best, disastrous at worst.

So then, begin to recognize that the edicts of the Court Royal may have coercive force, but they are not laws properly speaking. We may then comply with them, but we should not *obey* them. I am indebted to the Catholic philosopher Russell Hittinger for suggesting the difference. To comply is to refrain from disobeying. I believe that the Court Royal's outlawing of prayer in public schools was an egregious theft of authority from ordinary parents and teachers and a severe constriction of what it means to be a human being in society. To comply with the edict in this case would be to refrain from praying in school. But to *obey* would be to really heed the edict and take it into your mind and heart as possessing legitimate authority. It would be to "hear" the Court Royal's intentions and make them your own, with such consequences as we now see in most of the public schools: teachers who believe that even mentioning Jesus in a history class is to be abominated. *That* is not what the Court Royal said, but it flows from its clear animus against religion, its clear assumption that religion is necessarily divisive and not unitive; its clear aversion, we might say, to hearing the strains of hymns coming on an evening from the church on the green in the central square of the village.

So we should determine, at every pass, that though we may comply with this or that illegitimate edict, we will not be *obedient servants*. The Court Royal says that we may not begin the day with a prayer. That is clear. We will then make sure that religion forms a large and ancillary part of our study of the humanities: literature, history, and art, for obvious examples. We will let them take the opening prayer-pawn, and capture the rook instead. *Paradise Lost* is the greatest poem written in English. Well, we will be teaching *Paradise Lost*, and since you can never really teach a work of art unless you are to some extent in sympathy with it, we will have no qualms about asserting what we believe Milton has right.

Second, we should put to full use whatever liberty is still recognized, or act with liberty in areas upon which the Court Royal has not gotten around to encroaching. Take for example the sexual composition of social groups. The freedom to assemble—to form those social groups, not just for recreation or entertainment or drinking bouts, but for any human purpose whatever—is a fundamental freedom, flowing from the social nature of man. No government has any business intruding itself into the by-laws of a private organization. That freedom was abjured several decades ago, when the Courts Jester ruled that business groups like the Jaycees had to admit women. A truly freedom-loving people would have found the decision repugnant. Yet for some reason the Court did not touch the Shriners. In other words, the Court has been somewhat haphazard, and its inconsistency or inattention leaves us room for action.

For every all-male or all-female team or club or business organization that the Court neuters, we should establish three more, wearying our governing enemies with work or exasperating them with the obvious ineffectiveness of their measures.

So, for instance, the Court Royal decrees, with astonishing arbitrariness, that the area surrounding the entrance to an abortion clinic must be cordoned off as a speech-free zone. But why should the people of a town be compelled to allocate policemen to that zone, when the cops could be doing any number of other and more pressing things for the public good? Or suppose that the Court defends public displays of obscenity. Does the Court then also compel the people of a town to defend such displays, at their own expense? If the Court recognizes a right to offend, we can recognize in turn that those who are offended have a right to express their outrage, and not just in an editorial in a newspaper, either.

Third, we should try to revive social life on our own. Jabba the State wants to devour everything in sight, but even Jabba cannot conceivably do it. Nothing prevents us from coming together for the enjoyment of goods that our ancestors knew. This is especially true of the churches. Our betters, our managers, our keepers, our tax-masters, would like to exchange "freedom of religion" for "freedom of worship," with worship confined to the walls of a building, in self-imposed catacombs, to die out for want of brave witnesses. To hell with that. Literally: back to hell whence it came, the notion that the "free exercise of religion" is satisfied by pleasant rites held inside a church. Let the churches come out. Let pastors and congregations decide: for every single offense against the vigorous liberty of the church, we will walk and pray in two outdoor processions with the Sacrament, host two lectures, organize two summer picnics with Mass outdoors, march to the cemetery on Memorial Day, and in general be so merry and open, so solemn and cheerful, so rich in the beauty and the depth of our faith, that despite themselves people will look our way and want to share in the wine we are drinking.

TEN

Pilgrims, Returning Home

And so we come around again to the great division between ourselves and people who place all their hopes in the world, and are therefore always a skip of the heart away from despair.

Consider the wise name of John Bunyan's great allegory, *Pilgrim's Progress*. Bunyan took for granted that the only way to go forward is to be a pilgrim, because our true home is not here, no matter how deeply we love the world that God created, as we ought to, and the land of our birth. You have to have courage to embark upon the journey:

> He who would valiant be
> 'Gainst all disaster,
> Let him in constancy
> Follow the Master.
> There's no discouragement
> Shall make him once relent

His first avowed intent
To be a pilgrim.
Whoso beset him round
With dismal stories,
Do but themselves confound—
His strength the more is.
No foes shall stay his might,
Though he with giants fight,
He will make good his right
To be a pilgrim.

Bunyan's hero, Christian, meets along his way many a temptation to stay where he is: Mr. Worldly Wiseman, the secular fellow who is to be found in all ages, the know-it-all who tries to chill your spirit with a smile and a toss of the hand; or Vanity Fair, the shopping mall to be found in all ages, where you spend your days chasing after colorful and costly trifles and never get round to the pilgrimage at all. Christian is not Christian unless he is on the pilgrimage. "Come, let us be on our way," says Jesus, who declares Himself to be that very way we must travel.

The poets of the faith tell us the same. Dante discovers that he has lost his way in a dark wilderness, "in the middle of the journey of our life." His path up the sunlit mountain, "the origin and cause of every joy," is blocked by a lynx, a lion, and a wolf, allegorical beasts representing sins of lust, pride, and avarice, or the flesh, the devil, and the world. These beasts get the better of Dante not by rushing him with claw and fang but by reducing him to cowardice, acedia, and despair: "I lost all hope to gain the mountaintop." People think that they can advance themselves by means of wickedness or by keen attention to worldly things. It is like thinking that you can climb a mountain by taking a short cut through quicksand.

There was a time, in the United States, when the phrase "Christian progressive" meant that you wished to re-form social institutions according to the moral teachings of Christ, while keeping your eyes also upon the union with God for which man is made. A Christian progressive might battle to limit a man's working hours to fifty a week, not *primarily* because he believed that a man had no right to ask someone else to work sixty, but because families needed their fathers at home also. A Christian progressive might be wary about woman suffrage, not because he believed that women were foolish, but because he did not want the household to be supplanted by the individual as the fundamental unit of the society. But something happened: the international interference of Woodrow Wilson, the Bolshevik seizure of Russia, the socialist and bitterly anti-religious revolution in Mexico, the rise of neo-paganism in Germany and Italy, and soon enough Christian leaders were shedding the tenets of their faith. Instead of interpreting politics in the light of Christ, they began to interpret Christ in the light of politics.

Then it was that "progress" detached itself from the pilgrim. All Westerners are infected with the malady. We are all primed to suppose that life for our children must necessarily be better than life was for us. In part this supposition derives from the obvious advancement in the power of our tools, though, as I have said, we are in danger of becoming mere subjects or slaves of those same tools. But in large part it is a cheerful and blockheaded and simplistic replacement of the pilgrimage with something else entirely. The pilgrimage was the way of the Cross, but this way of "progress" is supposed to eliminate all suffering upon earth. The pilgrimage required you to bend your knee in penitence for your sins; this way of "progress" allows you to damn your ancestors and praise yourself for your enlightenment. The pilgrimage involved self-denial; this way of "progress" promises limitless self-indulgence. The pilgrimage brought those bittersweet and priceless moments of forgiveness, because every pilgrim knows that he is a sinner; this way of "progress" denies the sinfulness of those who submit to it and forgives *no deviation* from what is momentarily held to be correct. The pilgrim knows we have no lasting home on earth and turns his gaze toward heaven above; the progressive believes we have no lasting home in heaven, and turns his gaze toward earth, to make it a paradise by means of technology and sheer brute force.

The pilgrim can love the earth as well as it ought to be loved, forgiving its failings; the progressive hates the earth, because it never measures up to the engineered paradise he imagines. The pilgrim calls upon God; the progressive calls upon other men, whom he suspects or despises, then he calls upon technology, including the technology of government, and finally, when all of that breaks down, he calls upon wickedness itself. We will have paradise only when we have turned the world into hell, as Milton's Satan, the ultimate progressive of that sort, declares:

> So farewell hope, and, with hope, farewell fear;
> Farewell remorse! All good to me is lost;
> Evil, be thou my Good: by thee at least
> Divided empire with Heaven's King I hold
> By thee, and more than half perhaps shall reign,
> As Man ere long, and this new World, shall know.

The battle line between good and evil runs through every human heart, said Solzhenitsyn. Those who attempt to bleach the world of sin are sinners themselves, and the more ambitious they are, the more swaddled up in pride and ignorance they become. People who want to bring heaven upon earth have turned the earth into hell and made rivers run red with blood, because the first thing they must do is the one thing they cannot do, which is to cure themselves. If we are to be healed, we must walk the way of the Cross. The progressive cannot diagnose his own disease. But that does not mean that he rejects the way of the Cross entirely. *He makes everyone else walk it.* It is the rule of what the Catholic anthropologist René Girard tabs as the default position of mankind. Do not give up your lusts. Do not sacrifice yourself. Sacrifice the other. Other people *must be* to blame.

There is a further irony to note. The progressives of old had a clear idea of what they thought would bring about their earthly paradise: the dictatorship of the proletariat, the emancipation of women, the elimination of monarchy and its replacement with democracy, universal education, and so on. None of their nostrums has delivered on its promise, and some have had the perverse effect of rotting away the foundation upon which their suppositions of beneficence were based. So it is that democratic machinery without the soul of democracy has produced a far more intrusive and liberty-crushing state than anything that the proudest monarch could have imagined—or wished, since such constant political preoccupation would have left no time for boar hunting or chasing women. So it is that universal schooling has not brought Milton to the millions, but rather has taken Milton away from the brightest and replaced him with "young adult" junk. So it is that women have been emancipated from the freedom of the home and chained to salaried work and lives of relative loneliness.

The progressives of our time, however, no longer bother to tell us where they believe they are going. They neither know nor care. Having sown the wind, they reap the whirlwind and are at its mercy. The rudder has cracked and the ship knows no direction. At the moment the only liberty they believe in is the slavery of sexual license and the permission to fashion themselves in the image of any one of a multiplying number of sexual identities, whose very multiplicity and arbitrariness suggest how frail they are and how empty of meaning. What boon this is supposed to confer on mankind, or what this is supposed to contribute to the common good, progressives do not attempt to say. They cannot. In other words, the progressives of our time have no notion of a goal and therefore no notion of progress. They are not moving at all but sinking, deeper and deeper, into delusions and disappointment, blaming their failures on those who are insufficiently eager to sink along with them.

But we are pilgrims. We must remember that at all times. We are *on the way.*

Bearing the Mark of the Lord

"Do not conform yourselves to the world," says Saint Paul, "but be transformed in the working of your mind." We too were once lost, says Saint Peter, but now we have been saved, made into a royal priesthood, a people set apart by the Lord as His own. When the Lord sent Cain forth to wander east of Eden, that first murderer begged for protection, and so the Lord set a mark upon his forehead, the mark of Cain, so that anyone who raised his hand against Cain would suffer vengeance for it.

The mark on the forehead is, literally, a *character*. So also at the consummation of all things: John the Evangelist saw a great multitude marked with the sign of Christ. As the hymn puts it:

> Each newborn follower of the Crucified
> Bears on his brow the seal of Him who died.

"Remember, man, that thou art dust," says the priest on Ash Wednesday, as he signs the character of the cross in ashes upon the penitent, "and unto dust thou shalt return."

Keep it in mind. Say to yourselves and to your children, "We have been marked with the character of Christ. Not by our nature and not by our efforts, but by the grace of God we sinners have been marked as new creations. We must not walk in darkness anymore.

"We have been marked with the character of Christ. We will not play the futile games of the world. We will not fornicate, we will not divorce, we will not snuff out the lives of our children, we will not seek to filch the pleasure from sexual intercourse while neutering its effect. We will not put our money in the collection basket for what is lewd or obscene. If we fall, we will confess our sins and repent and bear the just chastisement. But we do not want these maddening lusts. We have other ways, much more human ways, to entertain ourselves.

"We have been marked with the character of Christ. We will not play the futile games of the world. We take care never to lie, never to mislead, never to commit the sin of detraction against our brothers. We check ourselves against parroting the lies of others. We refuse to wrest words away from plain reality. We will not inflate our language with vague abstractions so as to hide from ourselves and others what we are really up to. We will not turn words into totems, falling down before them, and begging 'democracy' or 'equality' or 'inclusivity' or whatever may be the current mumbo-jumbo to save us. We do not want to be foolish, so we do not speak the patois of those who have been fooled. We will not pretend to know what we do not know, or, what is more common in an age of governmental surveillance and force, *to pretend not to know what we do know, not to see what we see.*

"We have been marked with the character of Christ. We will not play the futile games of the world. We do not have other gods before God. We refuse to place our hope in magic 'science,' which amounts to placing our hope in *scientists*, who are men as we are: frail, vain, ambitious, stubborn in error, prone to going along with the herd, eager for power over others, apt to believe themselves to be wiser than they are. We will respect knowledge of the natural world exactly as such knowledge warrants, no less and certainly no more. We do not place our hope in magic 'democracy,' or magic 'government,' or magic 'equality,' or magic 'gender inclusivity,' or any other wave of the wand and rabbit pulled out of a top hat. We will honor legitimate authority, and we will obey just laws, but we will not bend the knee before knaves, ruffians, shrews, whores, butchers, and fools.

"We have been marked with the character of Christ. We will not play the futile games of the world. We take care not to lay up for ourselves treasures upon earth, where moth and rust corrupt and thieves break through and steal. When we ask ourselves what we want to be, the first thing we think of will not be what we will do to earn a salary. We will not make our families pay for our ambition. We will not make ourselves slaves to avarice. We will not make Sunday an asterisk in the week, the blip in between the supposedly real days of work. We keep holy the Lord's Day, not the weekend.

"We have been marked with the character of Christ. We will not play the futile games of the world. We honor the good, the true, and the beautiful. We do not envy them, we do not reduce them to mere words, we do not sneer at wise judgments and call them mere opinions. We do not run after the popular, which in the blink of an eye will have fallen into oblivion. We do not indulge ourselves in slovenliness and call it honesty. We will not praise what is drab and ugly and call it avant-garde or edgy or courageous.

"We have been marked with the character of Christ. Everything we do must bear that same character, even if sometimes in a light and gentle way. Our play, our work, our family life, our reading, our schools, our dances, our flirtations, our care of the sick, our neighborhoods, our bearing of children, our last moments as we bid the world farewell—everything.

"We must be clear about this. The world around us is not Christian. It is not even sanely pagan. It is quite mad and quite unhappy. We cannot minister to them by appearing to be pagan or by making ourselves half mad and half miserable. We can minister to them only by being sharply distinct. Those in the world who are weary of its broken promises will not listen to us if we speak the language of the world. They are longing for a different language entirely—the real language, which will restore to them the world's lost beauty and goodness and point them towards what is beyond the world. They do not want us to stretch ourselves out lazily among them. They want to join us *on the way*."

Getting Earth into the Bargain

If your aim is earth alone, says C. S. Lewis, you will lose it, but if you aim for heaven, you will get earth into the bargain. Consider one of the hard sayings of Jesus: "To those who have, more will be given; but from those who have not, even that little which they have will be taken away." If all your hope is in the world, you are like the man who sweated his life away filling his granaries and then, when they were full, said to himself that he would retire and live off his wealth. "Fool," said God, "even this night your life will be required of you." Vanity of vanities, saith the Preacher, all is vanity.

The Christian loves the world best by keeping it in its proper and subordinate place. For God has created nothing evil: "And God saw all that he had created, and behold, it was very good." No Christian is permitted to hate creation, for the Son of God himself deigned to take on human flesh and dwell among us, He through whom all things were made. Christ does not promise us eternal life in a disembodied soul, flitting about in spiritual space, a kind of nothing dwelling nowhere; He promises to raise us from the dead. "Have you had anything to eat?"

said the risen Lord to the disciples on the shore of the Sea of Galilee, as He was broiling a fish over a fire.

This is the promise of the Christian faith. Everything that we have loved in the flesh will be restored to us, cleansed, perfect, never to be lost, in that new heaven and new earth revealed to the apostle John when he saw the heavenly city, the new Jerusalem, descending from heaven like a bride adorned for her husband. When the pilgrim Dante wonders whether the blessed souls in heaven will be blessed even more fully once they are reunited with the flesh, he receives a resounding affirmative, as all the souls cry, "Amen,"

> maybe less for themselves than for their mamas,
> their fathers, and the others they held dear
> before they had become eternal flames.

That is the open secret that we all find so hard to learn. Love does not hoard itself up but gives freely, gives with abandon; so that he who seeks first of all to save his life shall lose it, but he who is willing to lose his life shall save it. The corollary for culture and civilization is clear enough. You cannot save a culture by raising culture to the ultimate good. That is what the sad prophet of culture Matthew Arnold tried to do, once he had lost the sunny liberal Christian faith of his father, Thomas Arnold, headmaster of Rugby. He believed that we would be saved from anarchy by being immersed in the best that has been thought and said and done. Ralph Waldo Emerson, the everlastingly optimistic American, believed much the same. It did not work out. Cut off from the springs of the divine, the best that has been thought and said loses all conviction, and the best that has been done seems utterly impossible ever to do again—as the cathedral of Chartres and the monastery at Mont-Saint-Michel seemed to the faith-starved Henry Adams.

He who would save a culture or a civilization must not seek first the culture or the civilization, but the Kingdom of God, and then all these other things, says Jesus, shall be given unto him as well. That is not simply a promise that a person believes or not but a revelation of the inner logic of a culture's being. Just as we cannot produce joy on an assembly line, or even seize joy by seeking it, but rather receive joy as a gift when we are seeking something greater than joy—when we give ourselves away in love—so we cannot produce culture except as it comes to us through our seeking what is higher than culture. "I will go in unto the altar of God," says the psalmist in Jerome's translation, "to God, who giveth joy to my youth." So too with culture.

The happy people of Europe celebrating the triduum of Corpus Christi had no notion that they were reviving the drama, an art form that had lain dormant for more than a thousand years, as they performed the rambunctious "mystery plays" on stages wheeled through villages from Lisbon to Prague, but that is in fact what they did, and they never would have done it if drama, not something else, had been their aim. The medieval painters who dwelt lovingly upon the countenances of Mary and the infant Jesus had no notion that they were giving to art an impetus that had been missing in it since the time of Aristotle and Alexander, the careful meditation upon the human face and figure, but that is what they did, and they never would have done it had their aim been a footnote in a textbook on art history and not something else. I imagine that Michelangelo would have found easier ways to earn a few pieces of gold than lying on his back on scaffolding a hundred feet in the air, pestered by the aging Pope Julius and suspicious of his rivals Bramante and Raphael below, but something moved him besides the solution of merely technical challenges. Take away the devotion and you take away the soul. The cynic and the agnostic are kissing cousins—if they can quit muttering long enough to kiss at all. The cynic and the agnostic achieve little, because they cannot fling themselves away in divine charity. They are too timid for that. Even their motto rings hollow: "Let us eat, drink, and be merry, for tomorrow we die." They eat and drink, but they are not particularly merry, and fearing that they will be slow in dying, and knowing no meaning either to suffering or to pleasure, they wish to conscript physicians themselves into the ranks of the executioners.

First things first.

A Good Land

I will end with a vision.

It is not a vision of something new in the world. It does not require science fiction devices that the world may never see, such as transporters that can move you in a moment from your living room to Oakland, assuming that you are so confused as to want to go there. It does not require remaking man according to the blueprint of some evil social engineer. It does not require spontaneous production of food from thin air, or of art and music from the brains of college professors. It does not require a global government, which is to say a global tyranny. It does not require some Quantum Leap Forward in education, so often promised and never delivered. It does not require saints; only such ordinary human beings whereof the good Lord has made so many.

Have you not sometimes wakened from a troubling and feverish dream to see after a few cloudy moments that you have not, after all, burned your house down, killed your teacher, fallen in a drunken stupor down an empty elevator shaft, been kidnapped and held bound by a leering sociopath, watched a recent television comedy, or lost your life's savings in a swindle? The relief you feel is accompanied by a clearing of the mind; the specters that troubled you vanish; you rub your eyes, shake your head, swear that you will not drink *that* again, and go about your daily business.

Something like that will one day happen to the Western world. Someday people will wake up and say, "Why did we believe such a mass of stupidities, cruelties, and lies? What was the point of it all?"

When that happens—and it must, because the truth will out—let them see what I see in my mind's eye, scattered everywhere across the land, havens of sanity and health, of reverence and wisdom, of good work and cheerful play, of marriages according to nature and nature's God, rich with children, and *knowing things*, the ordinary things, which will strike the newly wakened as wonders from another world altogether.

I see men and women who often enough get on one another's nerves, no doubt about that, yet who understand that each without the other is as half of a heart, half of a life. I see boys and girls teasing one another merrily, which they can do in full confidence, because innocence protects them from intending or supposing evil, and they grow up like olive shoots in a garden, straight and strong. I hear men praising the beauty and the wise ways of their wives, and women praising the courage and the intelligence of their husbands. I see boys and girls walking hand in hand again, and I see the cheeks of a lad flush with confusion and happiness when the girl he likes lets him walk her home. These are not sentimentalities. They are the great and real things, no less real for having been so long denied, despised, and forgotten.

I see schools filled with good books and ordinary teachers—who know the things they are supposed to teach, and who also love good books. I see people working with their hands again to make things of beauty, sewing a dress, planing a door, laying a stone wall, painting a postcard. I see people coming together to do ancient and human things: to sing, to dance, to play, to worship God. I see a neighborhood surrounded by wastes of idle poverty and idle wealth, like a wild lily springing up between the cracks of an abandoned walk.

I see children playing. Some of them are young and race around without a care in the world. They play baseball, jump rope, climb trees, go fishing, play cards, pick berries, ride bicycles, yell at each other, yell for each other, and while they are doing these things they have no notion of the open sewer that washes over the banks in places where other children live, infesting those lives with filth and corruption. They know none of the evil things that we place before the eyes of children now. They are growing in wisdom and stature. Because they are outdoors so much, their arms and faces are tanned, the muscles start out in their wrists and knees and neck, and they are altogether ready for sleep when night falls. They enjoy more of real life in a day than their poor rickety counterparts enjoy in a month.

I see other children, the elderly people who sit and watch their grandchildren playing. They have slipped most of the heavy cares of life, and now enjoy a kind of frolic old age, with contented hearts and glittering eyes. They do not take themselves very seriously. When the little boy runs up to his grandfather, he flings himself upon the old man, as if grandfather were a stout old oak tree, full of leaves and gnarly limbs and never to be moved. When the little girl runs up to him, he takes her by the hand and lets her lead him to her flower bed, as if he were an old shuffling ogre and she were the princess charming him back into life.

I see a church full of sinners who know they are sinners, so although the service is full of ceremony, the people do not stand on it—they take their worship seriously, but not themselves; and their worship is in any case filled with solemn play. They pray to the God who made them and redeemed them. They enjoy the virtue that brings man nearest to the freedom of God—gratitude. They know that the sweetest things in life are given and received, not earned and paid for. That is why they sing: for singing is what the lover does.

Is this an idyll? No, because the enemy still prowls about as a roaring lion, seeking whom to devour; sin waits at the door, and the fall of each day foreshadows the last. I am only describing what was and what may again be ordinary *human* life, with its ordinary joys and sorrows.

And the traveler, his ankles swollen and his brain filled with the feverish vision of evil things he wishes he had never seen, leaves the broad highway of the world and turns aside along a road he had once heard something about, though he had never actually set out upon it. Now he does. The police sirens, the cries of men maddened with envy and ambition, the shrill shrieking of women impossible to please, the fever of licentiousness, the human voices rendered ugly and brutish with lust, the fiery nettles of greed, the oppressive black smoke of boredom and disappointment—all these fade away, little by little, until the traveler can no longer tell if he still hears them, or was it just one locust scraping its wings in the dust?

Then he comes upon a small pond, where a boy sits, thoughtfully, skipping flat stones across the water. Before the traveler can say a single word, the boy turns to him with a wry smile and looks him in the eye.

"What took you so long?" he says.

About the Author

With more than a dozen books on topics ranging from literature and culture, education, spirituality, and theology, Anthony Esolen has earned a reputation as one of the most penetrating, pungent, and strikingly original writers of our time. A professor of English at Providence College, where he teaches Renaissance literature and the Development of Western Civilization, Dr. Esolen is a senior editor of *Touchstone* magazine and a regular contributor to *First Things*, *Crisis*, *The Public Discourse*, *The Catholic Thing*, and *Magnificat*. His critically acclaimed translation of Dante's *Divine Comedy* quickly became a standard for both university courses and popular readers. A graduate of Princeton University (B.A.) and the University of North Carolina (Ph.D.), Professor Esolen lives with his wife and children in Rhode Island.

Index

128, 134, 148, 160, 163–65, 171, 173–74

Muggeridge, Malcom, 16, 19

Murillo, Barolomé Esteban, 40, 128

music, 3, 7, 30, 35, 37, 39–40, 46, 54, 64, 69, 75, 87, 116, 119, 127, 138, 191

N

Nathanson, Bernard, 19

Nelick, Frank, 85

New Chastity and Other Arguments Against Women's Liberation, The, 124

Nineteen Eighty-Four, 15–16, 27

Nova Scotia, 38, 53

O

Odysseus, 167–70

Odyssey, the, 168, 170

Orwell, George, 15–16, 27, 56

Orwell Corners, 49, 54–56, 58, 62, 64, 67

Ottawa, Canada, 51, 63

P

Paradise Lost, 30, 86, 179

Pater, Walter, 75, 138

patriarchy, 103–5

Patrick Henry College, 80, 88

Pieper, Josef, 70, 130, 159

piety, 64, 75

pilgrims, 69, 181–85, 189

Pilgrim's Progress, 181

poetry, 6, 29–30, 34, 40, 43, 46, 50–51, 54, 78–79, 83, 86, 88, 102, 130

poets, 2, 4, 6, 13, 24, 28–31, 39–43, 70, 102, 142, 155, 182

polis, 161, 168–71, 173

politics, 1, 26, 28, 63, 65, 67, 71, 85, 88, 113–14, 117, 164, 170, 183

Pope, Alexander, 6, 31

pornography, 91, 96–97, 126, 142

Princeton University, 74, 76, 80

professors, 72, 75–80, 82–86, 88, 117–18, 174, 191

progressives, 85, 184–85

Prohibition, 113–14

Q

Quinn, Dennis, 85

R

reason, 73, 75, 176, 178

relativism, 75, 118

Rembrandt, 34, 40

Renaissance, the, 28, 39, 43, 46, 80, 100–2

Restoration of Christian Culture, The, 33

Rhode Island, 26, 142, 153

Robusti, Jacopo, 27